Frederick Haynes Newell

Water Supply for Irrigation

Frederick Haynes Newell

Water Supply for Irrigation

ISBN/EAN: 9783337141226

Printed in Europe, USA, Canada, Australia, Japan

Cover: Foto ©ninafisch / pixelio.de

More available books at **www.hansebooks.com**

DEPARTMENT OF THE INTERIOR—U. S. GEOLOGICAL SURVEY.

WATER SUPPLY FOR IRRIGATION.

By FREDERICK HAYNES NEWELL.

CONTENTS.

	Page.
Introduction	7
Preceding reports	7
Area irrigated	8
Area irrigable	9
Size of streams	10
Relative run-off	13
Fluctuations of rivers and lakes	15
Nonperiodic oscillations	18
Variations in precipitation	25
Subsurface waters	28
Cost and value of water supply	30
Principal drainage basins	31
Missouri river basin	34
Location and area	34
Elevation and topography	35
Land classification	35
Extent of irrigation	36
Water measurements	38
Precipitation	39
Gallatin river	41
Madison river	46
Jefferson river	49
Missouri valley	53
Prickly Pear valley	54
Dearborn and Sun rivers	55
Chestnut valley and Smith river	57
Teton and Marias rivers	59
Judith and Musselshell rivers	60
Milk river	62
Yellowstone river basin	63
Location	63
Area and topography	64
Area irrigated	65
Water measurements	65
Precipitation	67
Yellowstone river, above Bighorn	68
Bighorn river	69
Tongue river	70
Powder river	71
Lower Yellowstone river	72
Platte river basin	73
Location and area	73
Elevation and topography	74

CONTENTS.

	Page
Platte river basin—Continued.	
Land classification	75
Extent of irrigation	75
Water measurements	76
Precipitation	76
Upper North Platte	78
Laramie river	79
Lower North Platte	81
South Platte, above Denver	82
Cache la Poudre and other creeks	86
South Platte, below Greeley	90
Tables of mean monthly and annual discharge	91

ILLUSTRATIONS.

		Page.
Plate CVIII.	Map of the drainage basin of the Missouri river in Montana...	34
CIX.	Map of the drainage basin of the Yellowstone river............	64
CX.	Map of the drainage basin of the Platte river.................	74
Fig. 42.	Diagram of maximum, minimum, and mean discharges of western rivers...	11
43.	Diagram of discharges of large rivers of the United States.......	12
44.	Diagram showing relative size of drainage basins and depth of run-off...	13
45.	Diagram of periodic oscillations of water level...................	17
46.	Diagram of nonperiodic oscillations of various rivers and lakes..	21
47.	Diagram of nonperiodic oscillations of Colorado, King, and San Joaquin rivers..	22
48.	Diagram showing comparison of nonperiodic oscillations of the Great Lakes with Great Salt lake...................................	22
49.	Diagram of nonperiodic oscillations of the Great Lakes..........	23
50.	Diagram of the distribution of the mean monthly precipitation at sixteen stations in western United States	27
51.	Index map of large drainage basins...............................	32
52.	Diagram of mean monthly rainfall at four stations in the Missouri basin..	40
53.	Diagram of daily discharge of West Gallatin river below Spanish creek, Montana...	43
54.	Diagram of daily discharge of Madison river near Red Bluff, Montana...	48
55.	Diagram of daily discharge of Missouri river at Craig, Montana..	58
56.	Diagram of daily discharge of Yellowstone river near Horr, Montana..	66
57.	Diagram of daily fluctuations of North Platte river, Wyoming....	83
58.	Diagram of daily discharge of South Platte river near Deansbury, Colorado...	84
59.	Diagram of daily discharge of South Platte river at Denver, Colorado..	85
60.	Diagram of daily discharge of Clear creek, Colorado.............	86
61.	Diagram of daily discharge of North Boulder creek, Colorado....	87
62.	Diagram of daily discharge of St. Vrain creek, Colorado.........	88
63.	Diagram of daily discharge of Big Thompson creek, Colorado....	89

WATER SUPPLY FOR IRRIGATION.

BY F. H. NEWELL.

INTRODUCTION.

This report is the fourth in a series, each one of which relates to a certain extent to the hydrography of the arid regions, viz, to facts concerning the quantity and distribution of water. Since these papers give the results obtained at various stages of progress, the one which is issued last must necessarily refer to data previously published, and perhaps repeat or modify some of the former statements. Before entering upon the subject-matter of this paper reference should be made to the preceding discussions, which are contained, respectively, in the first, second, and third annual reports of the Irrigation Survey, these being also known as parts II of the Tenth, Eleventh, and Twelfth Annual Reports of the U. S. Geological Survey.

PRECEDING REPORTS.

In the first annual report of the Irrigation Survey, on page 19, a description is given of the organization of this branch of the work, and on pages 78 to 90 Capt. C. E. Dutton reports upon the methods of the investigation and briefly describes a few of the results then obtained. In the second report, on pages 1 to 110, are given more detailed descriptions of methods and instruments, and also of the localities at which stream measurements have been made, the character of each drainage basin being briefly noted. The results of stream measurements are also shown in tabular form convenient for reference.

The third annual report of the Irrigation Survey continues the discussion of the subject of water supply or hydrography of the arid regions, and gives the results of measurements and investigations obtained during the fiscal year ending June 30, 1891. General descriptions are also given of the topographic and other features of some of the drainage basins, the discussion of the Rio Grande and Gila basins being particularly detailed. The present report, continuing in a line similar to that pursued in the cases of the drainage basins just mentioned, describes with equal fullness other of the more important basins, and brings together all available information bearing upon the water supply.

AREA IRRIGATED.

The total area upon which crops were raised by irrigation was, according to the results obtained by the Eleventh Census, 3,631,381 acres, or 5,674.03 square miles. This applies to the year ending May 31, 1890, the census being taken during the following June. Comparing this area with the total land surface west of the one hundredth meridian, it is found to be approximately only four-tenths of 1 per cent. In other words, for every acre from which crops were obtained by irrigation there were nearly 250 acres of land most of which was not utilized in any way except for pasturage.

The area of the land surface of the United States west of the one hundredth meridian and between it and the Pacific ocean is 1,371,960 square miles, not including thirty-six counties of western Oregon and Washington. Within this great extent of country are nearly all possible combinations of soil and climate, ranging from the smooth, almost barren, plains with scanty vegetation to the high rough mountains, the peaks covered throughout the year with snow and the slopes clothed with thick forests. In a broad way four great classes of land may be distinguished, according to the amount of moisture received or the water supply available, as shown principally by the character of the vegetation.

The following table gives approximately the amount of land embraced in each of these great classes:

	Square miles.
Desert	100,000
Pasture	961,960
Firewood	180,000
Timber	130,000
Total	1,371,960

The desert land is that within which the water supply is so small that the cattle can not obtain sufficient for drinking purposes, and the vegetation is too scanty or uncertain to be of value for pasturage. The soil is often rich, and with water would produce large crops.

The second class embraces all the Great Plain region, which, owing to the prevailing aridity, is useful mainly as pasturage. The localities at which agriculture is possible are relatively of insignificant size, although of great importance in a grazing country. This class also includes the valley lands within the Rocky Mountain region and the rolling hills, on which native grasses grow.

The land containing firewood is mainly that fringing the timbered areas, being intermediate in character between the pasture land and the high rough forested slopes or plateaus. It includes also the precipitous hillsides found at an elevation too low to receive a large or constant supply of moisture, which in general falls upon the more heavily timbered areas.

The fourth class embraces the forested areas upon the high mountains, where the conditions are such that trees have been able to attain a size suitable for timber. A large part of this area has been burned over at different times, destroying timber whose value to the country can scarcely be estimated, and a relatively small number of the trees have been cut for lumber, to supply the growing needs of the settlers. The existence of this timber, however, indicates a condition of climate and soil widely different from that prevailing over the plains or pasture lands.

The irrigated and irrigable lands are mainly included within those divisions which in their natural state are considered as desert or pasture lands. In a broad way it may be said that fully nine-tenths of this area is covered with a fertile arable soil, which only lacks sufficient moisture in order to be of great value for agriculture. Out of this total of, in round numbers, over 610,000,000 acres there have been, according to the census, 3,631,381 acres, or less than six-tenths of one per cent, provided with a water supply sufficient to enable crops to be raised.

AREA IRRIGABLE.

The proportion of this desert or pasture land which can be brought under irrigation in future is dependent upon the thoroughness with which the water supply is utilized. It is obvious at the outset, however, that this proportion must be small, probably under 3 per cent, but its exact amount can be determined only when the available waters of the region have been accurately measured. This simple fact, namely, that the area irrigable is governed by the amount of water flowing in the streams, at various times of the year, is often overlooked or forgotten in popular discussions of the subject.

The greater part of the available water supply comes from the high mountains with precipitous slopes, a less quantity being discharged from foothills, and a still smaller quantity, irregular in time of occurrence, from valleys or plains. The results of measurements have shown that the average amount of water, taking one year with another, is seldom greater than 1 cubic foot per second or second-foot per square mile of elevated and steep catchment area. The total catchment of this character within the area under discussion has been ascertained to be 360,000 square miles. This includes the greater part of the areas designated as being covered by timber and firewood. From the remaining land, namely, the pasture and desert, there is very little water available for irrigation. Although there is a large amount of water falling upon these tracts, yet the conditions are such that streams valuable to agriculture are seldom formed, for the greater part of the moisture either sinks into the ground and is subsequently lost by evaporation, or, when coming in heavy showers, flows off in the streams whose beds are nearly or quite dry for the rest of the year, and thus is plentiful only at times when there is no need of irrigation.

Assuming that there is an average annual discharge of one second-foot from each of the 360,000 square miles, the total amount of water available for the supply of the 610,000,000 acres of pasture and desert lands above-mentioned is 360,000 second-feet. Much of this water, however, escapes into large rivers which have cut their channels so far beneath the general level of the arable lands that the waters can not be diverted, and therefore they must be considered as lost to agriculture. This is notably the case with many rivers in the drainage basin of the Colorado river, also to a great degree in that of the Columbia. The total amount available for irrigation is therefore to be diminished by the quantity lost in this manner.

The amount of water which can be saved by storage systems in the undulating and hilly country, or utilized by the conservation of water from springs or flowing wells, is a quantity even more uncertain than that flowing from the mountains, for in this case there are few general facts of broad application. It may be assumed, however, that this amount will not exceed the quantity lost in deep drainage channels, such as those of the Colorado and Columbia systems. Taking, therefore, the whole amount of water available in the arid region as 360,000 second-feet, the area of land which can be irrigated can be approximately ascertained by assuming a standard duty of water. If, for example, 1 second-foot flowing throughout the year will irrigate 100 acres, then the total irrigable area is approximately 36,000,000 acres, or about ten times that upon which crops were raised by irrigation in the census year. With an average water duty of 150 acres to the second-foot, the area irrigable will be 54,000,000 acres, and so on, according to the duty of water assumed.

SIZE OF STREAMS.

The relative amount of water discharged by various rivers of importance to irrigation is shown by the diagram, Fig. 42, which gives at a glance the size of these streams at times of high and low water, and also the average for one or two years or more. From this diagram may be inferred the acreage which possibly can be irrigated by each of these streams by assuming a standard duty of water. In this figure the names of the rivers are given in the space to the left, and to the right of each of these is a bar whose length indicates the quantity of water in the stream. The vertical lines give the quantity in cubic feet per second. For example, in the case of the first stream, the West Gallatin, the bar almost reaches the 4,000 line, indicating that the discharge fell under this amount, while in the case of the Missouri it was over 16,000. The black portion of the bar, by its length, indicates the minimum discharge of the stream for the time during which measurements were made, while the shaded portion, including the black, shows the average discharge. The total length of the bar, including the black, cross-hatched, and unshaded portions, indicates the maximum discharge.

SIZE OF STREAMS. 11

In the case of two of the streams shown in this diagram, the maximum discharge exceeds the amount which can be shown on the sheet, that of the Salt being 300,000 second-feet, requiring to show it a diagram containing seventeen times the space allowed on Fig. 42, and in

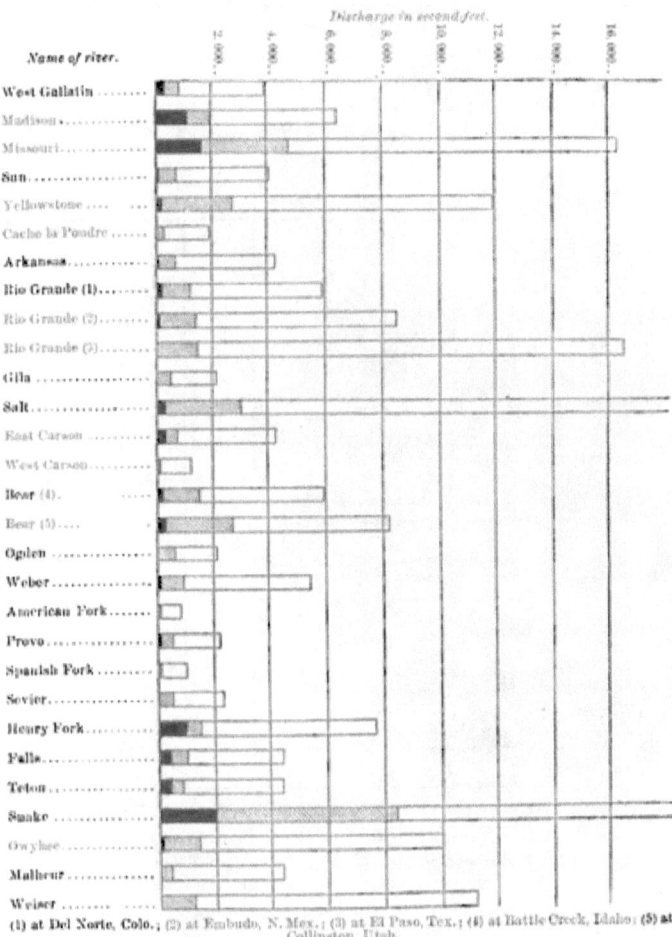

FIG. 42.—Diagram of maximum, minimum, and mean discharges of western rivers.

the case of the Snake 50,000 second-feet, or about three times the allotted space. In order to make a comparison between the streams of the arid region and some well-known rivers in the east, a second diagram,

Fig. 43, is introduced, showing similar facts, the scale, however, being much smaller. The relative change in scale can be seen by comparing the small space opposite the words "Upper Missouri" in Fig. 43 with the length of the line representing the same quantity in Fig. 42, this latter being the third line or bar from the top. In Fig. 43 the flood discharges of the Snake river at Idaho Falls, Idaho, and of the Salt river above Phœnix, Arizona, are shown in their relative proportions, the mean discharges being, however, scarcely perceptible on this diagram. The computations of discharge of Sacramento river apply to

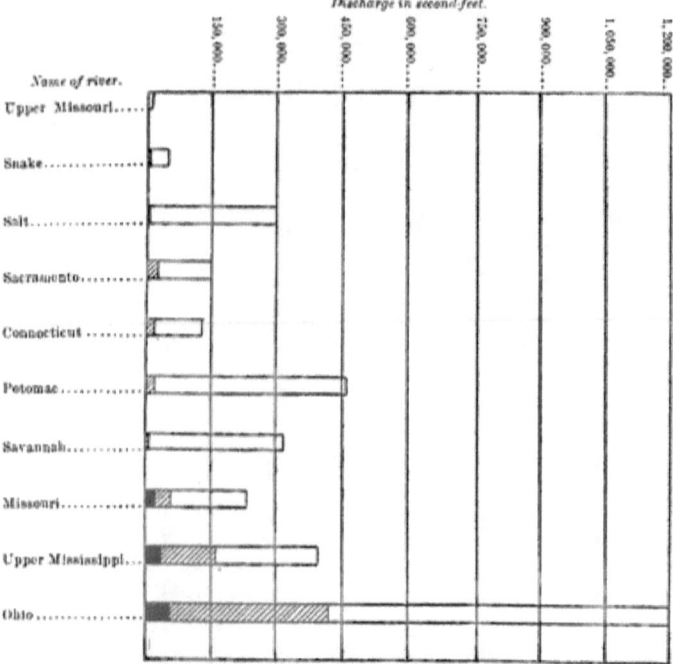

FIG. 43.—Diagram of discharges of large rivers of the United States.

the total outflow as determined by the state engineer of California. The remaining streams shown on Fig. 43, those in the eastern part of the country, were measured by officers of the Corps of Engineers, U. S. Army, except in the case of the Potomac, where gaugings were made by this Survey. The quantities shown on the diagram apply to the total discharge. The amount of water in the Mississippi at a point below the mouth of the Ohio would be represented by combining the three lines or bars at the bottom of the diagram. These three sets of values there shown, namely, for the Missouri, Upper Mississippi, and Ohio, represent strictly the discharges for the year 1882 only.

RELATIVE RUN-OFF.

The run-off, or quantity of water discharged per unit of area of the drainage basin, is exceedingly variable, being dependent upon the topography and climate of the drainage basin, each of these embracing too many details to be enumerated in full. The difference in quantity is illustrated by Fig. 44, which shows in a diagramatic form the relative size of the basins drained and the amount of water flowing from them in the course of the year. Each circle in this diagram represents by its size the area of the drainage basin named, the latter being, as a matter of fact, exceedingly irregular in outline. The black line or bar at the right of each circle gives by its length the relative depth of run-off, the unit adopted being the depth in inches per square mile

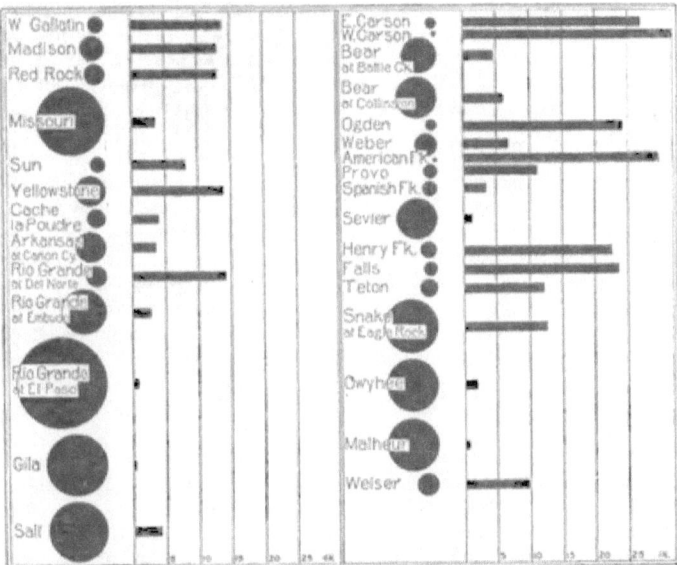

FIG. 44.—Diagram showing relative size of drainage basins and depth of run-off.

drained. The vertical lines indicate the number of inches; in the case of the West Gallatin, for example, a little less than 15 inches of water per year came from the drainage basin, or, in other words, if the water which flowed in the West Gallatin could be held without loss, it would cover a plain surface the size of the catchment area to a depth of less than 15 inches.

By the examination of this diagram, Fig. 44, it will be seen that as a rule the discharge per square mile is less from the large basins than from the smaller, or, in other words, the larger the basin the smaller the run-off. This is a fact noticed many years ago by engineers, and often recognized in computations of probable discharge of rivers based upon the area of the drainage basin and depth of rainfall. The decrease in run-off does not vary directly as the area of the basin, and for simplicity it has sometimes been taken as a function of the square root of the area. In this form it has been used in the formulas quoted in various works upon this subject.

The cause of the decrease in the proportion of run-off as a larger part of any drainage basin is taken is due principally to the fact that in the larger catchment areas there is usually included a greater percentage of level land, while in a small basin, embracing the headwaters of some stream, the catchment area may consist wholly of high, steep mountain slopes, upon which there is heavy precipitation and from which the water flows with great rapidity, the loss from evaporation being greatly reduced. This, for example, is the case in each instance shown in the diagram where the depth of run-off is great. The West Gallatin, Madison, and Redrock, the East and West Carson, and others have a catchment area composed almost exclusively of steep mountain slopes.

The decrease in depth of run-off with increase of area drained is shown in a striking manner in the case of the Rio Grande, the discharge of which beyond a point a short distance from the upper head waters increases but slightly, although the area tributary to the stream continues to grow larger and larger. In the case of this river, however, some allowance must be made for the peculiar condition of the drainage basin, embracing large catchment areas from which no water flows except in time of flood. In fact, as pointed out by R. T. Hill, the Rio Grande may be considered as a stream which has cut its way through a series of lost-river basins, and which, but for the outlet near El Paso, would be classified with the streams of the Great Interior basin.

There are occasional exceptions to the general rule that the average depth of run-off decreases as the basin grows larger; as, for example, in the case of the Bear, where, as shown by the diagram, the run-off at Collinston, below Cache valley, is greater than at Battle Creek, at the head of the same valley. This is due to the large run-off from the mountains on the east side of Cache valley, the topography being far more broken than at the head waters. The rule in this case will hold good if the streams from these mountains are considered as the main source of supply for the river and the water entering from other sources as tributary to these.

For convenience of reference the following table has been prepared, showing the mean annual run-off from several of the more important drainage basins, these being arranged in the order of proportion of discharge. This relation is expressed in this table not only in depth in inches, but also in second-feet per square mile drained, viz, the average discharge for the year in cubic feet per second is divided by the area in square miles from which the water comes. To obtain the depth in inches, it is necessary to multiply the second-feet per square mile by 13.575:

River.	Drainage area.	Run-off.	
		Depth.	Second-feet per square mile.
	Sq. miles.	Inches.	
West Carson	70	32·4	2·38
American Fork	66	30·0	2·22
East Carson	414	26·1	1·92
Ogden	360	25·0	1·84
Henry Fork	931	25·0	1·84
Falls	594	22·4	1·65
Snake	10,100	14·2	1·05
West Gallatin	850	14·0	1·03
Yellowstone	2,700	15·9	1·02
Truckee	1,549	12·9	·95
Madison	2,085	12·8	·95
Rio Grande at Del Norte	1,400	12·8	·95
Teton	967	12·1	·89
Provo	649	11·4	·84
Weiser	1,670	9·8	·72
Weber	1,090	8·3	·61
Sun	1,175	8·2	·61
Bear at Collinston	6,900	5·4	·40
Bear at Battle Creek	4,500	4·5	·33
Cache la Poudre	1,060	4·0	·30
Missouri	17,615	3·9	·29
Arkansas (6 years)	3,060	3·7	·27
Spanish Fork	670	3·5	·26
Average		13·8	1·01

As will be seen by this table, the depth of run-off varies greatly, ranging from over 32 inches in the case of the West Carson, which heads in the Sierra Nevadas, down to 3.5 inches for the Spanish Fork, whose catchment area is comparatively low and broad. The average of these **twenty-three cases is 13.8 inches, or at the rate of a trifle over 1 second-foot per square mile.** The catchments of these streams being well distributed throughout the mountainous area of the arid region, the average run-off as obtained in this way may be considered as being fairly representative of the discharge from the higher mountains of the West, and it has been used in this way in the preceding discussion.

FLUCTUATIONS OF RIVERS AND LAKES.

The average discharge, as discussed above, is a matter of first importance in considerations of water supply, but second only to it is a knowledge of the fluctuations which take place in the quantity delivered day by day or year by year. If the stream flowed at about a certain rate for long periods at a time or fluctuated with the seasons, returning to a former level each month, the subject of water control would be comparatively simple; but, unfortunately, the quantity of water flowing in a river is the resultant of so many variables, that it is impossible to predict with any degree of certainty what will be the amount flowing in the stream during the next crop season.

Farmers have learned by experience to estimate the possible discharge during the next succeeding crop season by the general appearance of the snows in the mountains, but beyond these rough approximations, as to whether the stream will be high or low, it is impossible to obtain definite knowledge. A study of the character of the fluctuations, however, which have taken place in past years throws light upon the probable behavior of the stream, and the longer such observations have been kept up the better able are the irrigators to judge of the probabilities.

The variation in the amount of water discharged day by day is shown graphically upon a number of plates published in the preceding annual reports, and also in a number of diagrams on the following pages. An examination of these diagrams shows that most of the rivers have a certain similarity in the character of the variation, namely, in that the water increases in amount during the late spring or early summer and then decreases to the minimum in September or October. This is the seasonal change which may be traced on nearly all diagrams of river height or discharge. Comparing the diagram for one year with that of another for the same stream, it is seen at a glance that although there is a certain similarity, yet no two actually coincide, the floods of one year coming earlier or later than those of another, and the total amount of water discharged differing by a large amount. There are thus, besides the change from day to day, two classes of fluctuations to be considered: First, the monthly or seasonal, which from its regularity may be called the periodic fluctuation, and second, the change from year to year, which from its great irregularity is known as the non-periodic oscillation.

The periodic oscillation or variation in height or quantity of water in rivers and lakes is a matter which can be readily determined by measurements carried on through a series of years. It follows in a general way the changes of temperature and is affected to a certain extent by variations in the amount of rain or snow fall; the relation in this latter case, however, not being one whose connection can be readily traced, except in the case of rivers similar to the Gila, receiving a great part of their waters from violent local storms. These rivers, however, can scarcely be said to have a periodic oscillation, although the storms are more apt to occur during certain months of the year. On Pl. LIX of the third irrigation report[1] a diagram is given, showing the periodic oscillation of four rivers in connection with the average rainfall at a typical station in the basin of each stream.

The periodic fluctuation of a number of important rivers and lakes of the United States is illustrated in Fig. 45, which shows in a generalized form the average height for a number of years. At the top is shown the average gauge height of the Missouri river at Yankton, S. Dak., and below this of the Cache la Poudre and Arkansas rivers near the point where they leave the mountains in Colorado. In the case of the

---

[1] Twelfth Ann. Rept. U. S. Geol. Survey. pt. 2, Irrigation p. 226.

first stream the rise to the June flood is rapid and the decline is gradual, while in the other two the June flood is more abrupt, the water falling nearly to the minimum in August. Below these is given the average gauge height of the Arkansas at Fort Smith, Ark., showing the difference in the behavior of the river at a point farther away from the mountains. Here floods prevail from February until June, then falling to low water in September or October. The early floods come from the lower

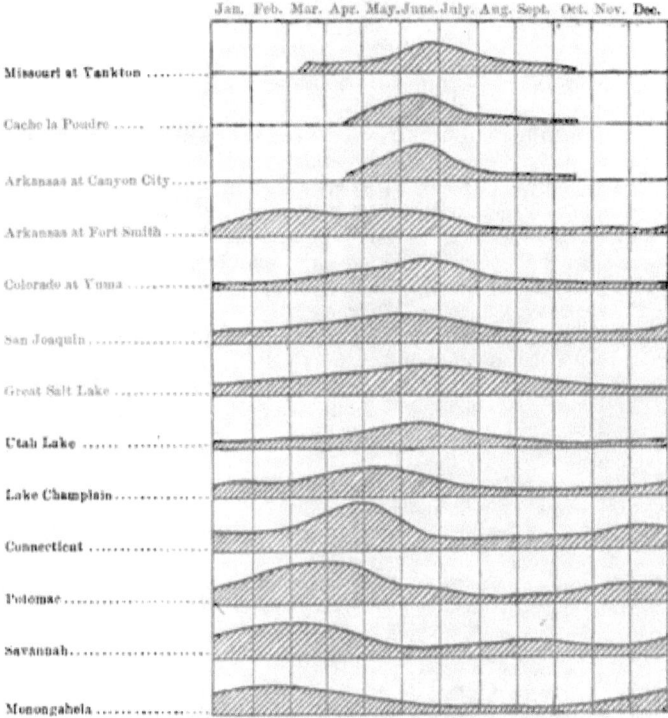

FIG. 45.—Diagram of periodic oscillations of water level.

plains region, and these are followed in turn by high water from more elevated portions of the basin, the head-water floods coming last of all.

The fifth figure from the top is that of the average gauge height of the Colorado river at Yuma, Arizona; the floods in this great stream culminating in June, as do those of the mountain streams of the arid region. Below this is the San Joaquin river of California, whose greatest discharge comes a little earlier in the season, the high water of winter beginning in December or even in November. The rise in both of these rivers is similar in many ways to that of Great Salt lake and

Utah lake, in Utah, the maximum in both of these occurring in June and the altitude of the surface falling gently toward winter. The last four diagrams on the page show the behavior of the principal Eastern rivers. This shows the later spring floods of the Northern rivers as compared with those farther South, the high water in the Savannah being earlier than in the Potomac and in the latter than in the Connecticut. The curve of river height of the Monongahela is typical of that for other tributaries of the Ohio.

NONPERIODIC OSCILLATIONS.

The nonperiodic oscillations give rise to the greatest concern on the part of the engineer and the irrigator, for while he can be reasonably certain regarding the character of the periodic variation he must at all times be on the watch for extraordinary occurrences for which there are no analogies. The rivers and lakes may for a time increase in volume or may apparently shrink so greatly as to cause serious alarm as to their permanence. In the humid regions these nonperiodic oscillations are of less moment, but in the arid regions, where water is always scarce, any change for the better or worse has an immediate effect upon the community as a whole.

The extent and character of nonperiodic oscillations may be illustrated by a few instances taken from streams in Colorado and other states. By reference to the table given below the average monthly discharge of the Cache la Poudre can be seen for the months from April to October inclusive for the years 1884 to 1891. This table shows that the average discharge for the seven months gradually decreased from 1,573 second-feet in 1884 to 373 second-feet in 1888, a decrease of 1,200 second-feet, or over three-quarters of the amount flowing in 1884. Since 1888 the discharge has increased, being in 1891 less than one-half that in the year first named. This, as can be imagined, is a most serious matter; for if streams are liable to shrink to a third or even a quarter of their value, the owners of the canals taking out the water, as well as the irrigators, must of necessity suffer.

Mean monthly discharge in second-feet of Cache la Poudre creek, Colorado.

Year	April	May	June	July	August	September	October	Average for seven months
1884	219	2,537	4,812	2,144	792	305	205	1,573
1885	447	1,419	2,910	1,857	656	272	202	1,109
1886	*300	1,309	1,876	717	338	185	129	693
1887	*200	*1,300	1,401	735	307	175	*120	605
1888	181	483	1,113	420	213	199	*90	373
1889	113	649	1,358	514	187	67	69	419
1890	200	1,944	1,280	649	287	103	80	520
1891	144	1,221	1,900	541	228	138	118	613
Mean	225	1,345	2,079	947	376	169	126	758

* Estimated.

NOTE.—These data, obtained for the most part from measurements made by the state engineer of Colorado, have been published in different form in the Twelfth Annual Report of the U. S. Geological Survey, part 2, irrigation, page 348. The interpolations given above, since they have been computed for the whole month, differ somewhat from the figures in the report named, these latter relating to portions of months only.

VARIATIONS IN DISCHARGE.

A fluctuation of a similar character, although not as decided, is shown by the Arkansas, whose drainage basin is farther south, but in many ways similar to that of the stream above mentioned. As shown by the following table, the average discharge in 1886 was 1,572 second-feet, and in 1889 was only 523 second-feet, or about one-third of the former amount. In succeeding years, however, the discharge increased, the average in 1891 being 1,382 second-feet, or about two and a half times that of 1889.

Mean monthly discharge in second-feet of the Arkansas river at Canyon City, Colorado.

Year.	April.	May.	June.	July.	August.	September.	October.	Average for 7 mos.
1886	*600	2,285	4,190	1,192	1,110	1,029	*600	1,572
1887	*450	*1,875	2,602	2,510	1,284	844	*600	1,452
1888	*1,000	1,440	2,090	1,350	902	605	*500	1,131
1889	300	606	1,374	602	346	220	233	523
1890	477	2,090	2,611	1,571	670	519	531	1,210
1891	857	2,012	3,221	1,468	954	473	624	1,382
1892	522	1,241	2,787	1,798	769	435	511	1,152
Mean	601	1,649	2,707	1,499	865	589	513	1,203

*The figures for 1886 and 1887 have been computed from the discharge measurements at Pueblo, allowance being made for the difference in drainage areas. See Eleventh Annual Report of the U. S. Geological Survey, part 2, Irrigation, pages 97-98; also Twelfth Annual Report, part 2, page 340.

That these oscillations, so strongly marked in the case of the Cache la Poudre and Arkansas, are not local may be seen by making comparisons with records of streams in other parts of the country. There are few rivers in the arid region, however, which afford records of considerable length, and the character of the oscillations can perhaps best be shown by records of the height of Utah lake, a fresh-water lake in Utah, and for a longer period by those for Great Salt lake, into which it empties. As shown by the following table Utah lake rose in height from 1884 to 1885 and then fell steadily until 1889, when it began to rise again. By comparison with the longer record of the height of Great Salt lake, it appears that this slight rise and continuous decline for a number of years are part of an irregular oscillation. The level of this latter lake has been falling, with occasional interruptions, for about fifteen years, this gradual decline being checked for a time by high water in 1885 and 1886.

Mean monthly height of Utah lake, Utah, above compromise line.

Year.	Jan.	Feb.	Mar.	Apr.	May.	June.	July.	Aug.	Sept.	Oct.	Nov.	Dec.	Annual.
	Feet.	Feet.	Feet.	Feet.	Feet.	Feet.	Feet.	Feet.	Feet.	Feet.	Feet.	Feet.	Feet.
1884	−0·7	−0·3	0·0	0·8	2·2	4·4	4·6	3·5	2·6	2·4	2·3	2·2	2·02
1885	2·4	2·6	2·5	2·7	3·4	4·2	3·9	3·4	2·6	2·2	2·1	2·1	2·82
1886	2·2	2·3	2·3	2·5	3·0	3·2	2·6	1·7	0·9	0·5	0·4	0·6	1·85
1887	0·8	0·9	0·9	0·8	1·0	1·2	0·9	0·0	−0·7	−1·1	−1·2	−1·1	0·20
1888	−0·8	−0·5	−0·1	0·0	−0·2	−0·7	−1·2	−1·5	−1·8	−2·1	−2·5	−2·6	−1·17
1889	−2·5	−2·2	−1·6	−1·3	−1·9	−2·4	−2·9	−3·3	−3·7	−4·1	−4·6	−3·3	−2·77
1890	−2·8	−2·2	−1·6	−1·1	−0·5	0·1	−0·4	−0·9	−1·2	−1·4	−1·5	−1·7	−1·27
1891	−1·7	−1·4	−0·8	−0·2	0·3	0·8	0·1	−0·5	−0·9	−1·2	−1·3	−1·2	−0·67
1892	−0·8	−0·1	0·2	0·2	0·3								
Means	−0·43	−0·19	0·23	0·46	1·35	0·95	0·26	−0·28	−0·69	−0·71	−0·62		−0·11

NOTE.—These data have been obtained from a survey of Utah Lake and from records kept by various individuals, notably James Aitken, Lake Shore, Utah county, Utah. All records have been reduced to compromise line, viz, an arbitrary height marked by two monuments, one near the mouth of Jordan river, the other near the mouth of the old channel of Spanish Fork. This height, when established in 1885, by agreement between the counties of Salt Lake and Utah was assumed to be 3 feet 3.5 inches above low water. (See also diagram of fluctuations in Twelfth Annual Report of the U. S. Geological Survey, part 2, Irrigation, page 336, Fig. 229.)

WATER SUPPLY FOR IRRIGATION.

Mean annual height of Great Salt lake, Utah, above Lake Shore zero.

Year.	Jan.	Feb.	Mar.	Apr.	May	June.	July.	Aug.	Sept.	Oct.	Nov.	Dec.	Annual.
	Feet.	Feet.	Feet.	Feet.	Feet.	Feet.	Feet.	Feet.	Feet.	Feet.	Feet.	Feet.	Feet.
1875									5.7	5.6	5.5	5.7	
1876	6.0	6.1	6.3	6.4	6.8	7.5	7.6	7.2	6.8	6.7	*6.6	*6.6	6.7
1877							7.3			6.1	5.8		6.0
1878	5.3	*5.9	6.0	*6.1	6.2	6.3	6.1	*5.8	*5.5	*5.2	4.8	4.7	5.7
1879					5.0						2.5	2.6	4.0
1880	2.7	2.8	2.8	2.9	3.2	3.3	3.2	2.8	2.3	1.9	1.7	1.7	2.6
1881	2.0	2.5	2.6	2.7	3.1	3.4	3.2	2.8	2.3	2.1	2.0	2.1	2.6
1882	2.2	2.3	2.4	2.6	2.9	2.6	2.6	2.3	1.7	1.4	1.4	1.4	2.2
1883	1.4	1.5	1.5	1.7	*1.8	*2.0	*2.1	*2.0	1.7	0.9	0.5	0.4	1.5
1884	0.4	0.5	0.8	1.2	1.8	2.5	2.8	2.5	2.4	2.3	2.2	2.3	1.8
1885	2.6	2.8	3.0	3.3	3.6	4.0	4.2	4.0	3.5	3.3	3.2	3.2	3.4
1886	3.5	3.8	4.1	4.3	4.5	4.6	4.2	*4.0	*3.8	3.6	3.4	3.6	3.9
1887	3.5	3.5	3.8	3.9	4.0	4.0	3.8	3.5	2.9	2.6	2.5	*2.5	3.4
1888	2.6	2.7	2.8	3.0	2.9	2.7	2.3	2.0	1.6	1.3	0.9	1.0	2.2
1889	1.0	1.2	1.5	1.2	1.2	0.9	0.3	—0.2	—1.0	—1.0	—0.9	—0.9	0.3
1890	—0.8	—0.4	0.0	0.2	0.7	1.0	0.8	0.5	0.0	—0.4	—0.4	—0.4	0.1
1891	—0.3	—0.3	0.0	0.1	0.3	0.4	0.1	—0.3	—0.5	—0.6	—0.7	—0.8	—0.2
Mean.	2.33	2.48	2.63	2.83	3.29	3.25	3.37	2.77	2.58	2.56	2.41	2.23	2.72

* Estimated.

NOTE.—The data from which the greater part of these figures have been obtained are to be found in Gilbert's Monograph on Lake Bonneville, pp. 233-238.

These facts are best shown by reference to Fig. 46, which gives in graphic form the averages of the mean values shown in the above four tables. The rapid decrease of water in each of the rivers and lakes just mentioned clearly appears, although the maximum and minimum points do not happen on the same years in each case. The longer record of Great Salt lake gives a hint as to what may have been the amount of water in Utah lake, and possibly in the streams during preceding years. According to this diagram the height of Great Salt lake has been as a whole steadily decreasing, but that this is only the latter part of a great fluctuation, a return from unusually high water to conditions more nearly normal, can be seen by referring to a diagram contained in Gilbert's monograph on Lake Bonneville.[1] According to this figure, the high water of 1876 is not far from the maximum for this century at least, while the low water of 1890 may be considered as being above the average height previous to 1865.

The most prominent feature shown in Fig. 46 is the unusually high water prevailing about 1885. This is a condition which has been noticed in many other localities, namely, that from 1884 to 1886 there was an extraordinarily large stream discharge and that lakes increased in height, in some localities the rise reaching its maximum in 1884, in others not until later. For comparison with the rivers of Colorado and the lakes of Utah just mentioned may be given the Colorado river and the San Joaquin, the former draining the western part of Colorado, the eastern half of Utah and nearly all of Arizona, and the latter receiving its waters from the western slope of the Sierra Nevadas. These, as will be seen by examination of Fig. 47, show a great rise in

---

[1] Lake Bonneville, by Grove Carl Gilbert, Washington. 1890. Mon. U. S. Geol. Survey, Vol. I, page 243, Fig. 33.

DECREASE OF WATER SUPPLY.

1884, followed by a decline more or less gradual and an increase toward the end of the decade. On this same diagram is given a curve, showing the variation in rainfall at all of the stations in the western part of the United States, where record has been kept for the past decade.

The average annual rainfall, as shown on Fig. 47, agrees quite closely

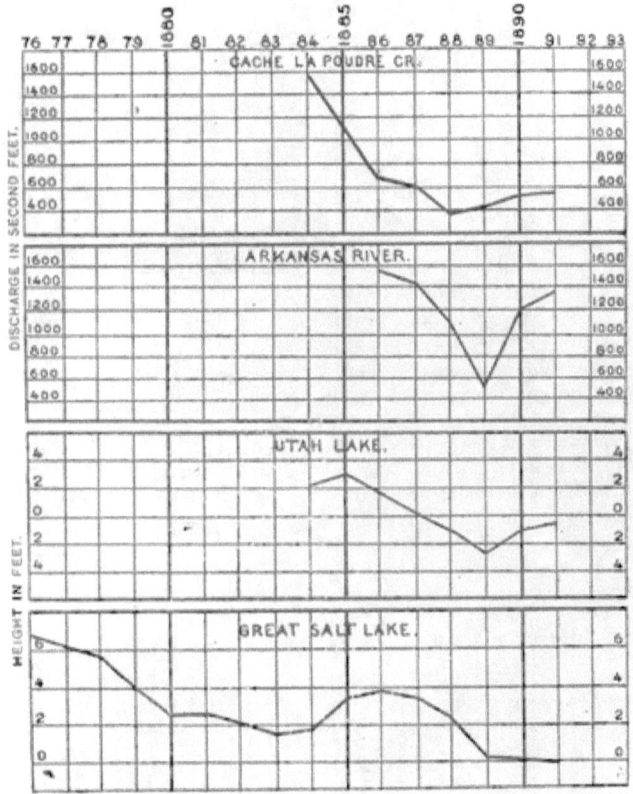

FIG. 46.—Diagram of nonperiodic oscillations of various rivers and lakes.

with the behavior of the rivers, more closely, in fact, than would have been anticipated. It shows that, taking the country as a whole, there was an extraordinary amount of precipitation during 1884. At about that time the great increase in rainfall was noticed and **popularly attributed to the effects of cultivation and to other causes under the control of man.** That these fluctuations in precipitation are widespread, and wholly remote from human influence even in the slightest degree, hardly needs discussion at present.

For comparison with the fluctuations of Great Salt lake it is interesting to note the average height of water in the Great Lakes, viz, Superior, Michigan, Erie, and Ontario, during the same years. This is given on Fig. 48, and an examination shows that in a minor degree there is a certain coincidence. For instance, there are in both cases times of relatively high water in 1870, 1877, and 1885–'87, after which date both fall. These points of agreement, however, are equaled or surpassed in importance by differences in the general form of the curve as a whole, Salt lake having unusually high water from 1870 to 1880, while the diagram for the Great Lakes shows almost the reverse. The important distinction in the two should not be overlooked, namely, that Great Salt lake has no outlet to discharge its excess water, while the Great Lakes have.

The nonperiodic variations in height in rivers and lakes, while taking place in humid regions, are not as generally noticed as in the case

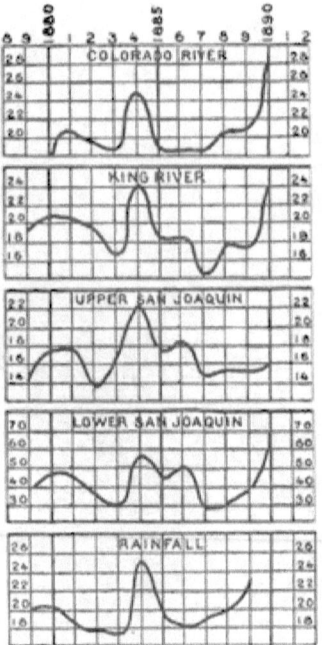

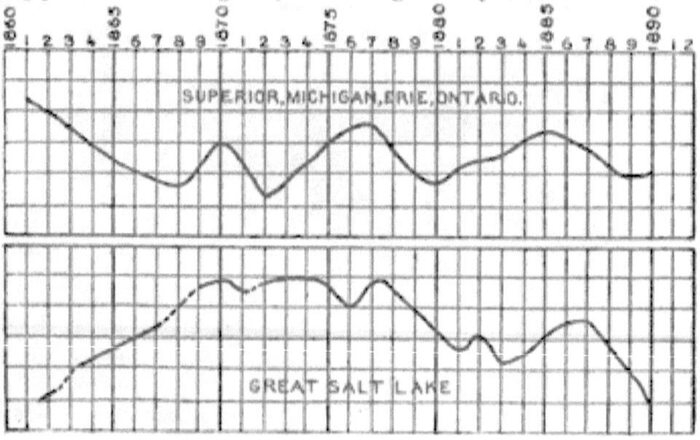

FIG. 47.—Diagram of nonperiodic oscillations of Colorado, King, and San Joaquin rivers.

FIG. 48.—Diagram showing comparison of nonperiodic oscillations of the Great Lakes with Great Salt lake.

of the waters of arid lands, because, water being far in excess of all demands, an increase or diminution passes unheeded by the public,

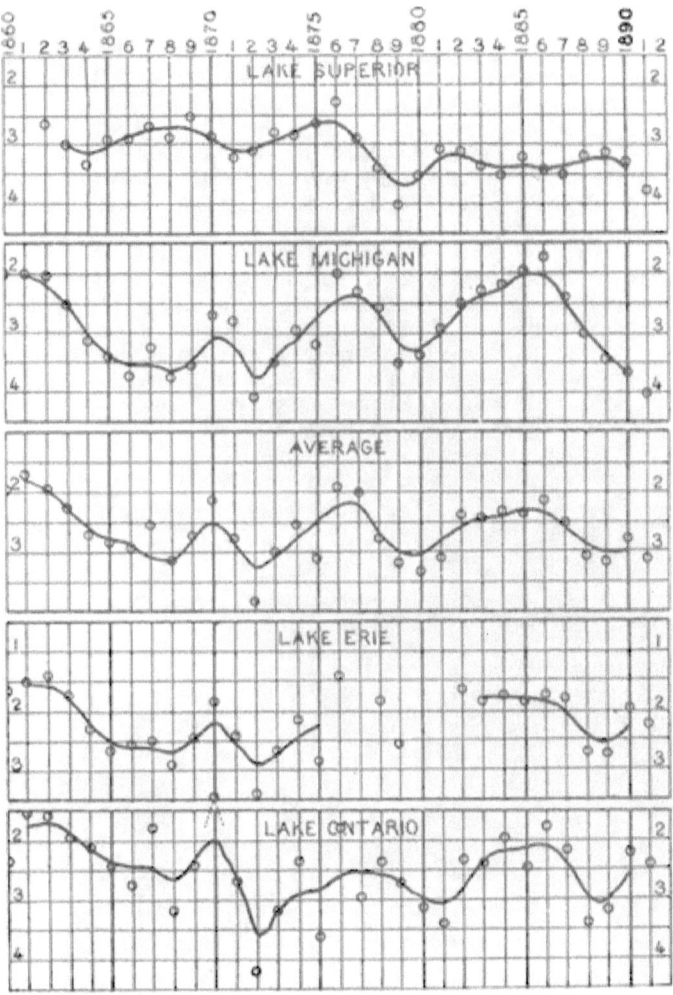

FIG. 49.—Diagram of nonperiodic oscillations of the Great Lakes.

although the same amount of change in the arid region would be of vital importance. Occasionally, however, circumstances occur by which these oscillations are forced upon public attention, as, for instance, in the case of Lake Michigan, which from 1879 rose steadily until 1886, and alarm was excited for the safety of the wharves and other property at Chicago. In the following years, however, the lake fell more rapidly than it rose, until in 1891 there was another alarm, but from the opposite cause, namely, that the lake was retreating so rapidly that it threatened to leave the wharves high and dry.

Observations have been kept of the height of the Great Lakes for over thirty years, giving one the best records of oscillations of water level in this country. It is instructive to examine this record, shown in the following table, in connection with the present subject, and to note the changes that have occurred during three decades. These facts are also on Fig. 49, which gives diagramatically the mean annual water level at stations on lakes Superior, Michigan, Erie, and Ontario, the small circles indicating the average height for the year noted at the top of the figure. The undulating line passing through some of these points is a smoothed-out curve, constructed by the use of the simple formula $b' = \frac{1}{4}(a + 2b + c)$, in which b' is the smoothed value for any year, a the observed value for the year preceding, b the observed value for the year under consideration, and c for the succeeding year:[1]

Mean annual height below plane of reference.

Year.	Superior.	Michigan.	Erie.	Ontario.	Mean.
	Feet.	Feet.	Feet.	Feet.	Feet.
1860		2.01	1.61	2.31	
1861		2.03	1.53	1.53	
1862	2.68	2.07	1.42	1.54	1.93
1863	3.02	2.54	1.71	1.94	2.30
1864	3.34	3.16	2.31	2.12	2.73
1865	2.93	3.40	2.67	2.38	2.85
1866	2.94	3.73	2.53	2.72	2.98
1867	2.72	3.29	2.50	1.77	2.57
1868	2.91	3.78	2.88	3.19	3.19
1869	2.58	3.66	2.46	2.34	2.76
1870	2.89	2.75	1.83	1.20	2.18
1871	3.25	2.82	2.42	2.63	2.78
1872	3.17	4.10	3.38	4.16	3.70
1873	2.84	3.45	2.67	3.09	3.01
1874	2.88	2.96	2.16	2.34	2.59
1875	2.75	3.21	2.83	3.63	3.11
1876	2.42	2.08	1.41	1.77	1.92
1877	2.87	2.31		2.96	
1878	3.37	2.62	1.82	2.36	2.54
1879	4.01	3.54	2.58	2.71	3.21
1880	3.55	3.40		3.11	
1881	3.10	2.88		3.42	
1882	3.14	2.51	1.63	2.38	2.41
1883	3.37	2.36	1.84	2.40	2.49
1884	3.51	2.26	1.77	1.95	2.37
1885	3.27	2.01	1.87	2.49	2.41
1886	3.45	1.77	1.76	1.57	2.19
1887	2.51	2.41	1.80	2.19	2.48
1888	3.22	3.03	2.49	3.37	3.03
1889	3.18	3.56	2.75	3.18	3.17
1890	3.31	3.68	2.05	2.23	2.82

[1] In this connection see preliminary report by Charles A. Schott on "Fluctuations in the Level of Lake Champlain and Average Height of its Surface above the Sea," Appendix No. 7, An. Rep. U. S. Coast and Geodetic Survey, 1887, p. 171.

Mean monthly height below plane of reference.

Month.	Superior.	Michigan.	Erie.	Ontario.	Mean.
	Feet.	Feet.	Feet.	Feet.	Feet.
January	3·44	3·35	2·42	3·08	3·07
February	3·65	3·31	2·49	3·06	3·13
March	3·79	3·15	2·30	2·84	3·00
April	3·62	2·94	1·83	2·26	2·66
May	3·22	2·69	1·51	1·83	2·31
June	2·96	2·45	1·35	1·68	2·11
July	2·71	2·37	1·39	1·74	2·05
August	2·62	2·43	1·55	2·02	2·16
September	2·61	2·62	1·80	2·41	2·36
October	2·66	2·84	2·11	2·79	2·60
November	2·85	3·09	2·34	3·06	2·84
December	3·20	3·20	2·39	3·09	3·00

This matter of the nonperiodic fluctuation of rivers and lakes and its connection with variations of precipitation has **been discussed by many writers** in connection with oscillations **of climate. The most elaborate discussion** of the subject is probably that **by Dr. Edward Brückner.**[1] In his work is given an elaborate discussion **of data concerning the** variations of rainfall and temperature, also **of wind movement and** other climatic factors, accompanied by diagrams exhibiting these **facts** in concise form. This volume has been preceded by pamphlets upon the oscillations of water level in the Caspian, the Black, and the Baltic seas in their relation to weather and on the question as to what **extent** is the present climate constant.

The principal fact taught by the examination of the fluctuations of the rivers and lakes of not **only** the arid regions, but **of the United States as a whole, is that these are due to** climatic forces, **not only continental, but even world-wide in extent.** It is no uncommon thing for a river to sink **to one-half of** its **average volume in any one year or double it the next. These matters, however, can not be regulated or affected, except perhaps in a very slight degree, by any action on the part of mankind. There is an idea widely current that the removal of the** forest cover at the head waters **of a stream acts injuriously in many ways and** causes greater fluctuations **in the quantity** discharged, especially in time of flood. This is a matter, however, exceedingly difficult to prove on account of this **enormous variation** in volume which takes place in every stream, whether in **a forested** country or not, **the** fluctuation due to climatic changes being enormously greater than that which can be attributed in any way to the result of forest destruction.

VARIATIONS IN PRECIPITATION.

The changes **in the amount of rainfall and snowfall at various localities** are by no **means comparable among themselves, one locality** showing a slight **increase in any one year and another a decrease; but,**

---

[1] Klimaschwankungen seit 1,700 nebst Bemerkungen über die Klimaschwankungen der Diluvialzeit, Von Dr. Eduard Brückner. Wien und Olmütz, Ed. Hölzel. 1890.

taking the averages of large numbers of observations, there are found to be, as before shown, certain general departures on one side or the other, one year being marked by an unusual amount of precipitation and another by deficiency. These averages of rainfall measurements do not agree as closely as might be expected with the statements of farmers as to droughts or good years, for they do not take into account the distribution of the rain by seasons; that is to say, there may be an unusual drought at the critical season of the year accompanied by great crop losses, and yet, taking the year as a whole, the deficiency of rainfall may not be especially notable. Therefore great reliance can not be placed upon the results of total annual rainfall measurements alone.

The attempt to connect the discharge of any one stream with the measurements of rainfall in the basin is unsatisfactory, unless the catchment area is unusually small and records of the rainfall have been kept at a large number of places well distributed over this area. This is a matter almost impossible of achievement in the arid region, where the greater part of the available water supply comes from high mountainous areas almost if not quite uninhabitable. Until this apparently impossible condition is fulfilled, namely, the keeping of many rainfall records in each catchment area, it will be hopeless to attempt to connect the rainfall and river flow in any detailed manner.

In a general way the average of the rainfall measurements over several states begins to show a coincidence with the fluctuations of the streams, although in detail the matter seems confused. This is shown in Fig. 47, as previously mentioned, and might be brought out in connection with change of level in many of the streams and lakes. The matter is one, however, concerning which the data at present available are still too limited for satisfactory discussion.

The periodic oscillations of rainfall throughout the year are capable of more satisfactory treatment than the fluctuations year by year, from the fact that there is a general agreement in stations near each other, changes in the distribution of rainfall by months being found to take place slowly as progress is made across the continent. A diagram therefore, prepared from a long record at any one station in one of the smaller states of the West, is found to be applicable in the main features to the greater part if not the whole area; that is to say, if May is the month of maximum rainfall at any one point it probably is for all localities in the state, while in the localities adjoining it is highly probable that the time of maximum rainfall will be either immediately before or after that of the given state.

Fig. 50 has been prepared to show the average distribution of precipitation by months at a few stations in the western half of the United States. It brings out in sharp contrast the differences in the character of the rainfall on opposite sides of the arid region. On the Pacific coast summer droughts are the rule, while on the eastern side of the arid region the greater part of the rainfall is during summer. Between these two the gradual transition from one to the other is well marked in nearly every instance. This matter of the characteristic distribution of precipitation throughout the year has been systematically discussed by Gen. A. W Greely in his report upon irrigation and water storage in the arid regions,[1] and also in a paper presented before the National Geographic Society upon rainfall types of the United States.[2] He points out that there are several distinct and simple types of rainfall, each of which can be represented graphically by a curve with a single bend or inflection, the average monthly amount of precipitation increas-

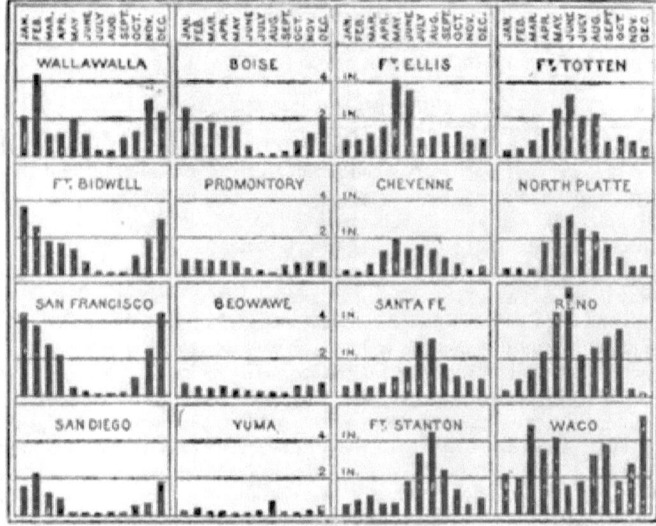

FIG. 50.—Diagram of the distribution of the mean monthly precipitation at sixteen stations in western United States.

ing steadily from a minimum to a maximum and then diminishing in unbroken progression. Each of these simple types of rainfall is shown to have some relation to the movement of winds from some one great body of water—the Pacific Ocean, the Gulf of California, the Gulf of Mexico, etc. Besides these simple curves are composite types, shown graphically by two inflections, there being in each a primary and a secondary minimum and maximum.

The diagram, Fig. 50, shows at least three of the simple types and several of the composite forms. In the cases of the portions of the dia-

[1] Fifty-first Congress, second session, House of Representatives, Ex. Doc. No. 287, Washington, 1891. Report on the climatology of the arid regions of the United States with reference to irrigation. By Gen. A. W. Greely, Chief Signal Officer, U. S. Army.
[2] The National Geographic Magazine, Vol. v. pp. 45-60. Rainfall types of the United States. Annual Report, by Vice-President Greely.

gram illustrating the distribution of precipitation at Fort Bidwell and San Francisco a general curve might be sketched connecting the tops of the small columns. This would represent fairly well the Pacific type of rainfall, which is characterized by heavy precipitation during the winter and prolonged droughts in summer. In a similar way a curve drawn through the part of the diagram for Santa Fe would represent the Mexican type, which is notable for the very heavy precipitation in August. The third simple type is perhaps best shown on this diagram by the conditions at North Platte, Nebraska. This has been named the Missouri type, from the fact that it obtains throughout the watershed of the Missouri River and its principal tributaries. As shown by the diagram, the rainfall during the winter is very light, the greatest amount of precipitation being in late spring and early summer.

SUBSURFACE WATERS.

The water obtained from rocks beneath the general surface of the country, although relatively small in amount when compared with that from streams, has great importance, from the fact that dependence must necessarily be placed upon this in many localities where running water can not be had. Not only is agriculture benefited indirectly by water from wells convenient for household use and stock purposes, but in many instances a supply sufficiently great for irrigation in a small way has been obtained. Water for irrigation is lifted from the wells generally by means of windmills or by machinery driven by steam or horse-power. In some localities the structure of the rocks is such that water rises to the surface and overflows, artesian wells being obtained by drilling to depths ranging from a hundred to a thousand feet or more.

The total number of artesian wells in the western part of the United States in 1890 was 8,097, as ascertained by the census of that year. These were found in North and South Dakota, Nebraska, Kansas, and Texas, and the states and territories to the west of these to the Pacific coast. Of this number, 3,930 were employed to a greater or less extent in irrigation, watering 51,896 acres, or 1.43 per cent of the total area irrigated. The residue of the wells were undoubtedly of benefit to agriculture to some extent; their principal value, however, being in the fact that they furnished supplies for municipal and domestic purposes, and also for cattle when the wells are in the vicinity of grazing lands.

No statistics have been obtained concerning the ordinary wells from which water is pumped or drawn by various means, but there is found in nearly every locality water saturating porous rocks near the surface in all places except on desert areas. On the Great Plains, for example, in western Nebraska and Kansas, it is sometimes necessary to go to depths of from 100 to 300 feet or more before water-bearing strata are reached, but throughout the arid region as a rule wells are successfully dug to a less depth. The widespread occurrence of water in pervious layers of the earth's crust, and sometimes in such quantities as to appear almost inexhaustible, has given rise to the notion that it flows in great channels very much as do the rivers of the surface, but covered from sight by rocks and soils. There are a few instances where underground watercourses actually occur, but these are extremely rare and are extraordinary in their nature, being found only in the great limestone deposits or among the lava flows of recently extinct volcanic regions.

In a majority of cases subsurface water occurs merely as moisture saturating the rocks. If these are unconsolidated and porous the quantity of water contained in the interstices is in the aggregate very large, while in the case of the hard compact granites or slate the proportion is extremely small. That all rocks which form the crust of the earth contain a certain amount of water can usually be shown by drying any of them and noting the loss in weight. The sands and gravels washed down from adjacent heights and filling depressions are particularly well adapted to hold moisture, and it is from these, as is well known, that the greatest quantities of water are obtained.

The behavior of the waters in these sands is still a matter of inquiry, and is not clearly understood. For instance, one leading question is: Are these stationary, or do they flow freely from place to place? It is probable that to a certain degree both of these conditions are found in nature. In a small valley entirely inclosed the water accumulates in the sands until they are saturated and the moisture approaching the surface of the soil begins to be evaporated. The matter then adjusts itself until a balance is reached between the amount which flows in and that which is evaporated, the level of water rising until the loss is equal to the inflow. If a well be made in this sand basin and the water drawn upon, the level of moisture in the immediate vicinity of the well is immediately lowered. The influence extends only with great slowness towards the edge of the basin, however, the water level not as a whole falling at once, as would be the case in drawing from a large open body, the place of the water removed from the center being slowly occupied by a gradual progression of moisture from the sides.

Instead of a small basin, if one of indefinite size be considered, there is seen a condition of things similar to that which takes place in a broad extent of country. The moisture at the lower limit of a large plain escaping either in springs or by evaporation is gradually replaced by the slowly progressing water, which percolates with a rate varying with the fineness of the rock or sand layer. The amount of water which can be taken from underground sources is limited not so much by the total quantity in the area, as by the rate at which it can flow through these sands or gravels, and after the first wells have drawn upon the supply already stored in the immediate vicinity the amount which can be taken afterwards is governed by the speed with which the moisture can progress to the place from ever-widening limits. In lost river basins and on low lands in the vicinity of irrigated areas the amount and behavior of this subsurface water becomes a factor of great local importance.

Popular interest, especially in the subhumid regions, has been aroused concerning subsurface or ground waters, and statements as to their distribution, quantity, and availability, especially for irrigation, have been eagerly received. The somewhat misleading and indefinite term "underflow" has been applied to these waters, and many persons awakening for the first time to a realization of their presence have received exaggerated impressions or have magnified the importance of phenomena previously known to engineers and geologists. Extravagant reports have been made as to the results of rude experiments, and many persons have been induced to believe that it was practicable to irrigate large portions of the subhumid region by means of the ground waters conducted to the surface of the gently sloping plains through long tunnels or open channels. Acting on this belief, thousands or even hundreds of thousands of dollars were expended, mainly in the years 1890 and 1891, in the construction of such projects, principally along or in the valleys of the Platte and Arkansas rivers. So far as can be ascertained by examination and measurement none of these projects can be said to be successful, although in a number of cases small quantities of water are obtained from the long, deep channels which penetrate the pervious beds of sand and gravel.

In each of the instances of these so-called underflow canals the level of the ground water, or what is known to engineers as the water table, is lowered in the immediate vicinity of the cut or excavation, and the upper part of the pervious beds being drained, a new slope of the water table is found, this being adjusted to the altered conditions. The progress of the water down this new slope is, so far as can be ascertained, practically constant, except as modified by local rains and changes of temperature. The quantity of water actually obtained, although large in one sense, as, for example, when compared with that from an ordinary well or the amount utilized for domestic supply, is almost insignificant with reference to the irrigation of any considerable body of land. The projectors of these irrigating schemes often failed to appreciate not only the fact that ground waters must in their very nature move slowly, but also that even in comparatively humid countries large volumes of water are necessary to conduct irrigation on an extended scale.

COST AND VALUE OF WATER SUPPLY.

The average first cost of water for irrigation throughout western United States has been ascertained to be at the rate of $8.15 per acre, while its value, wherever the rights can be transferred without the land, is $26. Applying these figures to the total acreage as ascertained by the last census, the total first cost of irrigating the lands from which crops were obtained in 1889 was $29,611,000, and the total value of the water rights was $94,412,000, the increase of value being $64,801,000, or 218.84 per cent of the investment. This latter sum may be taken as representing the value of the supply utilized. The average annual expense of maintaining the water supply was $1.07 per acre, or an aggregate of $3,794,000, this being the amount expended in keeping the canals and ditches in repair and free from sediment.

The estimated first cost of the irrigated lands from which crops were obtained in 1889 was $77,490,000, and their present value, including improvements, $296,850,000, showing an increased value of $219,360,000, or 283.08 per cent of the investment in the land, not taking into consideration the water. The average value of the crops raised was $14.89 per acre, or a total of $53,057,000. These figures have been introduced to exhibit the cost and value of irrigation in the arid regions. The value of the unutilized water supply can scarcely be estimated until more accurate information is obtained concerning the total amount of water and the acreage that it can be made to cover. By making certain assumptions, however, a rough estimate can be arrived at.

Taking the average first cost of water at $8.15 per acre and its present value at $26 per acre, the difference, $17.85, may be assumed as the value of the water as it flows in the stream. If 1 cubic foot per second will water 100 acres, then the value of 1 second-foot is $1,785. Taking the figures given on page 10, as to the total quantity of water probably available, viz, 360,000 second-feet, the total value of this water is $642,600,000. These figures obviously have no claim to accuracy, but merely indicate that, calculated on the most conservative basis, the water supply of the arid country must be ranked among the most important of its undeveloped mineral resources.

PRINCIPAL DRAINAGE BASINS.

In order to enter upon a detailed discussion of the water supply of the arid region it is necessary to consider the different portions in turn, and for this purpose the best method of grouping the facts is by natural divisions, viz, by drainage basins. The political divisions into states and counties unfortunately do not coincide with lines of drainage, except in a few instances, so that the discussion of water supply according to these arbitrary lines is less satisfactory than by the way first mentioned. The small map (Fig. 51) shows the relative location and area of the larger drainage basins of the west and their position with reference to the states and territories, the size of these in square miles being shown in the accompanying table, page 33. According to this table the total area of the part of the United States west of the 100th meridian is 1,380,175 square miles, not including thirty-six counties in the western portion of Oregon and Washington, the aggregate area of these, including water surface, being 61,840 square miles. Adding this amount, the total area of the land and water surface west of the 100th meridian is 1,442,015 square miles. The thirty-six western counties of Oregon and Washington above mentioned have been deducted because of the fact that in a study of water supply and irrigation it has been found convenient to omit from consideration these comparatively well-watered areas. The 1,380,175 square miles above mentioned include the area of several large lakes, the principal of these

Fig. 51.—Index map of large drainage basins.

being in Utah, California, and Montana. The aggregate area of these water surfaces is 8,215 square miles, which being deducted gives the total area of land surface used on page 33.[1]

The order usually adopted is that by which the head waters are first considered and then the tributaries in succession. The large drainage

---

[1] The areas of States and counties are those given by Henry Gannett, geographer of the Eleventh Census, in census bulletin No. 23, January 21, 1891.

AREA OF DRAINAGE BASINS.

Area in square miles of principal drainage basins by states.

Drainage basin.	Total.	Arizona.	California.	Colorado.	Idaho.	Kansas.[a]	Montana.	Nebraska.[a]	Nevada.	New Mexico.	North Dakota.[a]	Oregon.[b]	South Dakota.	Texas.[c]	Utah.	Washington.[d]	Wyoming.
Total area including water surface.	1,200,175	113,020	158,360	103,925	84,800	82,850	146,080	75,800	110,700	122,580	40,050	70,528	40,840	114,970	84,970	82,842	97,800
Upper Missouri	81,778						81,038										760
Yellowstone	69,683						36,212										33,121
Cheyenne, etc.[e]	114,300						3,750	17,910			250		60,840				12,050
Platte (North and South)								10,850			29,770						24,240
Kansas	57,320				10,790			7,040									
Arkansas	22,672			22,250	7,040					16,900				18,920			
Canadian	37,760			8,382	5,110					72,380				15,300			
Red	40,630			39,729										59,530			
Rio Grande, etc.[b]	15,800																
Green above Grand	100,457			7,527											15,916		20,977
Grand above Green	47,225			10,332											3,873		
Lower Colorado, etc.	26,167			22,294											21,633		
Gila and small West River basin	114,115	56,182	8,619	5,490					3,200	19,000							
Great basin	71,138	56,838								14,300		18,950			63,548		1,494
Sacramento and San Joaquin	218,872		47,240						102,729								
South coast, California	63,675		63,030		3,420							635					
North coast, California	21,740		21,740														
Southwest Oregon[f]	17,750		17,750														
Snake	8,880				72,380				5,280			8,680				6,682	5,298
Columbia in Montana, Idaho, and Washington[g]	108,080						25,000					12,650					
Columbia in Oregon[h]	50,040				7,880							24,063				26,160	
	24,063																

[a] West of the 100th meridian.
[b] Not including fifteen western counties.
[c] West of the 100th meridian and with part of Oklahoma.
[d] Not including twenty-one western counties.
[e] 12,315 square miles in Canada to be added.
[f] With various streams west of 100th meridian, including Moose, Little Missouri, Cheyenne, White, Niobrara, etc.

[g] North Platte, in Colorado, 2,025 square miles; South Platte, in Colorado, 20,205 square miles.
[h] Including Pecos and all drainage in Texas west of 100th meridian.
[i] Including all of Colorado river drainage in Utah, Arizona, and Colorado, excepting Green, Grand, and Gila basins.
[j] Coast drainage, mainly of Klamath river.
[k] Excepting Snake river drainage.

basins in this and preceding reports are taken in this general order wherever applicable, and from the east toward the west, as shown in the table. In this report the drainage basin of the Missouri, Yellowstone and Platte will be described.

MISSOURI RIVER BASIN.

LOCATION AND AREA.

The Missouri basin, as the term is used in reports concerning the arid region, usually includes the area tributary to the river of that name above the junction of the Yellowstone. As a matter of fact, the drainage basins of the Yellowstone, Little Missouri, Cheyenne, Platte, and other rivers form parts of the great basin of the Missouri river, but since each of these streams flows nearly to or beyond the limits of the arid region before uniting their waters in this great drainage system, it is more convenient to consider them as independent basins and at the same time to apply the name "Missouri" to the head water catchment area of that stream.

The total area of this basin is 95,093 square miles, of which 13,315 square miles, or 14 per cent, is within the Dominion of Canada, leaving 81,778 square miles, all in the state of Montana, with the exception of a few square miles in the Yellowstone National park. In this discussion of the water supply and the condition of irrigation reference is made only to the portion of the basin in Montana, few facts being available concerning the part in Canada. The boundaries of Montana have been laid out in such a manner that they include not only the greater part of the Missouri basin, but also in the southeast a portion of the Yellowstone basin, and on the west a large part of Clarke fork of the Columbia. The state line west of the Yellowstone National park follows for a portion of its course the rim of the basin, but with this single exception it has been located with reference to arbitrary lines rather than with regard to natural divisions.

The drainage basin of the Missouri, as shown by Pl. CVIII, is bounded on the west and southwest by the main range of the Rocky mountains, which forms the continental divide, separating the waters of the Missouri from those of the Columbia. On the southwest, where this divide forms the state line between Montana and Idaho, it separates the basin from the head waters of Snake river, or, as it was formerly known, Lewis fork of the Columbia. Further to the north, beyond the point where the Bitterroot mountains separate from the Rockies, these latter form the watershed between the Missouri and Clarke fork of the Columbia. Thus the Missouri basin is bounded on the south by the Yellowstone, a part of which is in Montana, on the southwest by the Snake basin in the state of Idaho, and on the west by Clarke fork in Montana.

ELEVATION AND TOPOGRAPHY.

The basin as a whole slopes toward the north and east, the highest ground, as shown by Pl. CVIII, being in the southwestern corner and along the western edge. The waters flow, therefore, in a general northerly and easterly course, leaving the basin not far from the northeastern corner. The rim of the basin is sharply defined in the higher portion, but in the eastern half, where the divides are low and rolling, the watershed is formed by prairie country, and therefore must be arbitrarily designated.

By means of the contours given on Pl. CVIII an estimate has been prepared of the area of the basin at **various elevations.** From an inspection of this table, given below, it **is apparent that over one-half of the basin is at an elevation below 4,000 feet.** In fact, the altitude is far less than it is popularly supposed to **be.**

	Square miles.
Total area in Montana	81,778
Area under 2,000 feet	618
Area from 2,000 to 3,000 feet	26,068
Area from 3,000 to 4,000 feet	22,317
Area from 4,000 to 5,000 feet	13,314
Area from 5,000 to 7,000 feet	13,218
Area over 7,000 feet	6,243

LAND CLASSIFICATION.

The small map on Pl. CVIII **shows not only the general** elevation of various parts of the basin, but, by means of the color, the general character of the **lands within this area. Three general divisions have been made based** upon the size or kind of the vegetation as determined by climate and **altitude. The darkest shade indicates in a broad way the relative location of the** forests or timber **land, while the lighter green shows the** area covered to a greater or **less extent by scattered trees, suitable for** firewood, occasionally **furnishing material for purposes of fencing. The remainder of the** basin, **colored a light brown, supports** a scanty vegetation, and, for the most **part, may be** considered as pas**ture** land, including under this designation vast tracts whose soil is arable, and which, with **an** abundant water supply, would produce large crops.

Dividing the total area of **the Missouri basin in Montana, viz, 81,728** square miles, into **these three classes, it has been found that there are** in arable or pasture **land, approximately, 64,398 square miles, in land more or less covered with scattering firewood 10,640 square** miles, leaving for the timbered **land 6,740 square miles. These designations are** largely arbitrary, for **there is, unquestionably, good pasturage within** the areas designated **as being covered with timber** or firewood, and, on the other hand, **there are trees and shrubs of value to the farmer scat-**

tered along all of the principal streams in the eastern end of the State. There is little, if any, agricultural land within the areas covered in whole or part by trees, most of this being rough broken land or high mountains.

The arable and pasture lands shown on the map include the localities where agriculture is carried on, or where the soil is such that it could be developed. Unfortunately, however, as shown by the character of the vegetation, the rainfall is deficient and farming can not be successful without the artificial application of water. It has been found that in the census year ending May 31, 1890, crops were raised by irrigation upon 234,036 acres, or 365·7 square miles. This is only 0·57 per cent of the total area designated above as arable or pasture lands. The localities at which irrigation was carried on in the census year are shown by the dark spots on the map, Pl. CVIII.

Besides the irrigated portions of the arable or pasture lands, there are along the rivers many thousands of acres which by a careful utilization of the water supply can be brought under cultivation. The extent to which agriculture can be developed is, however, dependent wholly upon the thoroughness of the conservation of the flood waters and upon the degree to which the large rivers are utilized. The area irrigable, while governed somewhat by the topography, is controlled by the manner in which the water supply is employed. It is not possible, therefore, to make any rigid distinction between the irrigable lands and the arable or pasture lands, but on the small map the attempt is made to show by a darker shade the relative area and location of the lands which, under the best circumstances, can possibly be reclaimed by irrigation. The area thus colored aggregates in round numbers 1,000,000 acres, or 1,562 square miles.

EXTENT OF IRRIGATION.

The acreage irrigated in the Missouri basin, as above stated, aggregated 234,036 acres. This includes chiefly the area from which crops were obtained during the census year. The areas colored dark green on the small map are found mainly in the western and southern part of the basin near the points where the smaller tributaries issue from the mountains and flow out into the first open valleys. Agriculture by means of irrigation has already developed to such an extent that all of the streams which can be readily diverted, by one or two farmers or a number of neighbors acting in partnership, have been utilized nearly to their full extent during the summer season, and there remains little water unappropriated except that which flows during the spring floods.

While on the one hand the demand for water has already exceeded the supply along the upper valleys of the Missouri, farther down, on the main river, there is a large amount flowing at all times of the year. Unfortunately, however, it is extremely difficult, if not impossible, to bring this water out upon **the vast extent of arable land, owing to the** steepness of the banks and the comparatively **slight fall of the stream.** There is thus a striking contrast between the condition of affairs in the **eastern** and western ends of the basin. In the latter locality are small **streams with** steep slopes flowing through comparatively narrow valleys, **the** water being widely distributed in the innumerable creeks, **while in eastern** Montana the water supply is all concentrated in the main **rivers and** the arable lands lie in great blocks embracing thousands of square miles.

The population is located mainly in the **southwestern portion of the** basin in the valleys among the mountains. **This is** due **to the fact that** the principal industry is mining, carried on in the canyons or **gulches** and among the crystalline rocks which contain the precious metals. **If,** however, the only industry **were** agriculture, this portion of **the basin** would still be the most prosperous and thickly settled, from the fact that the small streams in the mountains are widely distributed and the waters can be readily brought under control by the efforts of individuals or of companies. There is one peculiarity of the topography of this part of the basin which should be mentioned, namely, the bench lands **which** are found in each valley between the foothills and the narrow bottoms along the streams. These bench lands, although sometimes having gravel upon the surface, are usually very fertile, and as a rule surpass in excellence the lower lands along the bottoms of the valleys. They are usually cut by deep, narrow ravines, or coulees, as they are locally known, formed by the action of tributaries entering the main stream.

These bench **lands are remnants of** the beds deposited in former times from lake **waters before the rivers had** cut their present outlets. The streams **leaving each valley** pass through narrow canyons eroded **by the** flowing waters. Before these canyons were cut, the waters **being held** back, the material washed **from** the mountain was deposited, partially filling the deep basins. Gradually, however, the escaping water wore down the outlets until the bottoms of these lakes were laid bare, and continuing its downward course each stream cut trenches in the lake bottoms, in which the streams now flow. Thus each important stream in the western end of the basin flows at some distance below the general level of the bench lands, and its waters can be diverted with ease only upon the narrow flood plain. The principal problem presented to the irrigation engineer in this part of Montana is that of taking the water from the larger streams out upon these rich **lands.** The matter is complicated by the fact that they are deeply cut **by the** coulees traversing them **at short** distances, and also by the condition of development of irrigation, **viz, the** fact that many of the **improvements** made **at present** stand in **the way of** more comprehensive schemes.

WATER MEASUREMENTS.

The localities at which stream measurements have been made by this survey and the results obtained have been described in previous annual reports of the irrigation survey.[1] Some additional data have been obtained since the preparation of the last report and are presented herewith, together with a brief resume of the materials available for study of the fluctuations of water supply.

The three rivers, the Gallatin, Madison, and Jefferson, which unite to form the Missouri, have been measured at different times by the Geological Survey and by the Missouri River Commission. Continuous records of discharge have been computed for the Gallatin above Gallatin valley, and for the Madison near Red Bluff, while in the Jefferson basin Redrock creek alone has been observed for a series of months. A few measurements have been made on the Jefferson near Willow creek; that on August 19, 1889, giving a discharge of 202 second-feet, and on October 15, 1889, near Three Forks, 333 second-feet. Single measurements have also been made of some of the streams tributary to the Jefferson, viz, Ruby creek, Blacktail Deer creek, also Beaverhead and Bighole rivers, as noted in the following pages.

Several measurements have been made of the Madison near its mouth, that on August 17, 1889, at Blacks giving a discharge of 1,104 second-feet, and that of October 14, 1889, at Three Forks 1,191 second-feet. Considerable difficulty has been found in obtaining the discharges of the three rivers near their junction, on account of the fact that they divide into a number of channels and the height of the water in one stream affects the others for a considerable distance above.

Below the point at which the Gallatin, Madison, and Jefferson rivers unite a number of measurements have been made, showing that the discharge, as obtained by gaugings, has varied from about 2,500 second-feet up to over 8,500 second-feet. The seasonal fluctuations undoubtedly cause a variation both below and above these figures.

Besides the gauging stations of the Geological Survey at Toston, Canyon Ferry and Craig, described in former reports, records of the height of the water have been kept by the Missouri River Commission at a number of places, as shown by the following list, which includes all known data.

At Gallaher's Ferry, about 200 yards above the mouth of the Gallatin river, the height of the river has been recorded from August to November, 1890.

At Gallatin, Montana, records of river height have been kept from July to December, 1890. A measurement made at this point on August 6, 1890, gave a discharge of 2,640 second-feet. (In the Twelfth Ann. Rept., pt. 2, p. 237, this is erroneously given as 2,460 second-feet.)

---

[1] United States Geological Survey, Eleventh Ann. Rept., pt. 2, 1889-'90, Washington, 1891, pp. 36-43, 93-94, 107; also Twelfth Ann. Rept., pt. 2, 1890-'91, pp. 236-238, 346-347.

At Toston, about 30 miles below Three Forks, **the** Geological Survey made six measurements from April 8 to July 26, 1890, the results being shown on page 42 of the second annual report on irrigation. **The Missouri** River Commission kept records of height from **August 16, 1890,** to February 28, 1891. The elevation of low water **of 1890 at this place** was about 3,879 feet.

At Townsend, 43 miles more or less below Three Forks, a permanent gauge was established October 1, 1891, **by** the Missouri River Commission.

At Canyon Ferry, **about 18** miles from Helena, gaugings were made by the Geological Survey, giving the discharge for September, October, and November, 1889. A measurement made **on** September 18, 1890, by the Missouri River Commission near Canyon Ferry gave a discharge of 2,682 second-feet. The elevation of low **water was** in **1890** approximately 3,629 feet.

At French Bar, 71 **miles below Three** Forks, **the** discharge, as **measured** by T. P. Roberts on July 31, 1872, was 10,000 second-feet.

At Stubbs Ferry, which is given as being 73 miles from Three **Forks** a gauging was made in 1882 by the Missouri River Commission, **showing** a discharge of 3,770 second-feet. The records **of** river height have **been** kept from July, 1890, to January 17, 1891.

At Craig, a locality above the mouth of the Dearborn river, a gauging station was established by **the** Geological Survey and continued in operation through **1891.** The elevation of low water of 1890, as determined by levelings **made** by the Missouri River Commission, was about 3,629 feet.

At Great **Falls, Montana, records of river height were** kept from September **to December, 1890, by the Missouri River** Commission, and possibly **have been continued by the water-power** company at that **place.**

At Fort Benton gaugings have been kept with more or less regularity from 1873 to 1876 and from 1881 to 1890. In August of this latter year **a** permanent station was established, taking as zero the low water of 1889. The daily gauge height from 1873 to 1876 has **been** published in lithographed form by Prof. Thomas Russell, of the Weather Bureau.[1]

PRECIPITATION.

Measurements of the amount **of** precipitation have been **made at a number of points** within this basin by the Signal Service **of the U. S. Army, some of the records** being continued for **over fifteen years. The results** of these measurements show that the rainfall, **as measured at the** various stations, varies from 10 to 20 inches, **the average being about 15 inches, the greater** part occurring **in the months of May and June.** The following list gives the names and location of the more

---

[1] Stages of the Mississippi and of its principal tributaries, 1860 to 1889, pt. 2, pp. 217-220.

important of these stations, with the length of time during which observations were made, and the mean annual rainfall as derived from records furnished by the Signal Service.

Locality.	Length of record.	Depth of rainfall.
	Years.	Inches.
Fort Ellis, near Bozeman	15	19·6
Virginia, Madison county	9	16·0
Helena, Lewis and Clarke county	11	14·3
Fort Logan, head waters of Smith river	8	14·4
Piegan, head waters of Marias river	2	21·2
Fort Shaw, on Sun river	17	10·2
Fort Benton, mouth of Teton river	16	13·3
Fort Assiniboine, on Milk river	9	15·0
Fort Maginnis, near Judith mountains	7	16·6
Galpin, near mouth of Milk river	1	6·7
Poplar river	7	10·5
Fort Buford, mouth of Yellowstone	23	12·3

These localities are mainly in the valleys or on the plains, and therefore the results of the measurements do not represent the rainfall and snowfall upon the high mountains, which undoubtedly is considerably greater. It is safe to assume that the precipitation upon the summits is at least from 20 to 30 inches, and upon the valley lands of the western part of the Missouri basin at from 15 to 20 inches. In the eastern end of the basin, however, as shown by the measurements at Poplar river and Fort Buford, the rainfall rarely amounts to over 15 inches, ranging usually from 10 to 12 inches in depth.

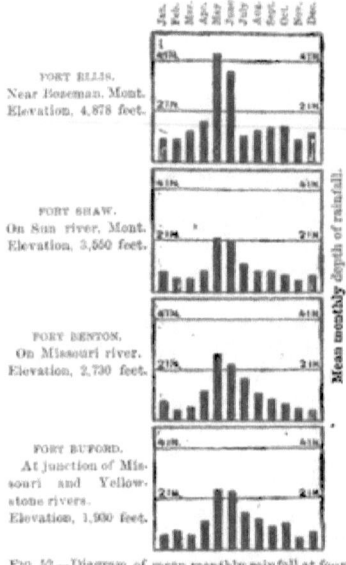

FIG. 52.—Diagram of mean monthly rainfall at four stations in the Missouri basin.

The amount of rain falling in any one year may vary widely from the averages given in this statement, which nevertheless serve to indicate in a general way the distribution of precipitation over the basin. The variation from year to year is exceedingly irregular, but comparing one year with another, it appears from the records that there was a general decrease during the latter part of the decade, the depth of rainfall in 1889 and 1890 being at most stations below the average.

The distribution of the precipitation by months is shown graphically on Fig. 52, the results at four stations having the longest record being selected. These averages, although obtained from widely separated localities, have a similar appearance in that the greatest precipitation is in the month of May, followed by a slight decrease in June. During the remaining months of the year, however, there is a decided range in the proportion of rain falling, in the case of Fort Benton, **for example, there** being a gradual decrease to the end of the year, **while at other** stations there is great irregularity.

The distribution of **rain** throughout the year is shown by the following **table, which gives the** average precipitation per month as obtained **from** the stations named on page 40, and also gives the percentage of the amount for the **year:**

	Inches	Per cent.
January	0·81	6·1
February	0·65	4·9
March	0·82	6·1
April	1·02	7·7
May	2·51	18·8
June	2·10	15·7
July	1·29	9·7
August	1·00	7·2
September	1·03	7·7
October	0·85	6·4
November	0·58	4·3
December	0·66	4·9
Total	13·35	100·0

This peculiar distribution of the rainfall is in itself favorable to agriculture, for, taking the months of May, June, and July as the principal part of the growing season, it appears that in an ordinary year over one-third of the rain falls during **these months, and thus, although the** rainfall is as a whole deficient, yet what there **is comes at the time when** it will do the most good.

With this brief summary of the principal facts concerning **the basin** as a whole, a more detailed description of the water supply in each sub-basin **is** given in the following pages, taking these in order from the head waters down, beginning with the Gallatin, Madison, and **Jefferson, and** preserving in general the geographic order.

GALLATIN RIVER.

The Gallatin river rises in the high mountains **in the northwestern** corner of the Yellowstone National park and in the ranges north of this. The river flows in a general northerly course through a succession of narrow valleys and canyons for a distance of about 50 miles from its head waters, finally entering the Gallatin valley, one of the finest agricultural areas in Montana, or **even in any of** the western states. At the lower end of this valley the stream receives the waters of the East Gallatin, which drains the short range **of the same name.** The small tributaries coming from these mountains unite near the base and flow in a general northwesterly direction along the eastern side of the Gallatin valley. At a distance of about 10 miles below the **mouth of the East** Gallatin the main stream enters the **Missouri.**

WATER SUPPLY FOR IRRIGATION.

The water supply of the Gallatin valley is peculiarly favorable to irrigation, and this, with the rich soil and temperate climate, has rendered possible a high state of agricultural development. On the eastern side of the valley is Bozeman, and a number of smaller towns are scattered about. The small streams coming in from the east and south have enabled irrigators to bring under cultivation large areas of crops at moderate expenditure of labor, and as these convenient sources of supply have been utilized in turn and population increased, they have rendered possible the construction of large systems of irrigation deriving water from the principal river, the West Gallatin. Thus by the distribution of small streams irrigation has grown rapidly and without interfering greatly with the thorough utilization of the magnificent water supply.

As has been previously stated, the amount of water entering the Gallatin valley by means of the main stream has been measured at a station below the mouth of Spanish creek near where the river leaves the canyon. The total area drained is 850 square miles, most of this being high, steep, mountain areas heavily covered with timber. The run-off, therefore, is unusually large, being from 13 to 14 inches in depth over the whole basin; that is to say, if the water flowing from this drainage area during one year were put back upon a plain of the same size it would cover it to the depth of 13 or 14 inches. The average rainfall is not known, but probably can not be much less than 30 inches. If this be the case the run-off represents nearly one-half of the precipitation upon the catchment area.

The discharge of the stream has varied from 320 to 6,800 second-feet, the average for three years being over 950 second-feet. This is equivalent to an average discharge of 1·12 second-foot for each square mile drained, the amount varying at different times of the year from about four-tenths of a second-foot up to 8 second-feet per square mile. This rate of run-off is probably greater than that from the East Gallatin range, from the fact that the topography in the latter case is less favorable to rapid discharge of the precipitation.

In Fig. 53 is given the daily discharge of the West Gallatin river at the gauging station previously mentioned from May, 1891, to the middle of July, 1892, with the exception of the month of April, 1892. As will be seen by the inspection of the diagram, the flood discharge of 1892 was far greater than that of 1891, this latter being represented by the lighter line. The diagram is not sufficiently high to show the maximum point, 6,800 second-feet, reached in June, 1892. Comparison should be made with the diagram on Pl. LX, in the Twelfth Annual Report, giving the discharge at this station from 1889 to 1891.[1] On this plate the discharge for 1891 represented by a dotted line, is seen to be somewhat less than the discharge for 1890, this latter, however, being decidedly

---

[1] U. S. Geol. Survey, Twelfth Ann. Rept., pt. 2, Irrigation, p. 228.

lower than the quantity shown on Fig. 53. This difference is best exhibited by the table of mean monthly and annual discharge shown on page 98, where the mean annual discharges for 1890, 1891, and 1892 are respectively 871, 880, and 1,123 second-feet. The rapid fluctuations shown on the diagram as taking place during time of high water are undoubtedly due largely to changes of temperature.

Taking the mean annual discharge of the West Gallatin as 950 second-feet, this, with a water duty of 100 acres to the second-foot, should irrigate 95,000 acres. It would be necessary, however, to store a large part of this water in order to make it available. By complete systems of storage and careful use of the water this duty could be somewhat

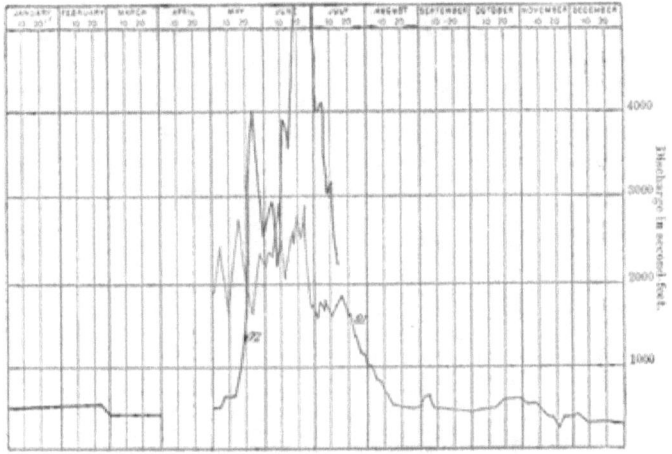

FIG. 53.—Diagram of daily discharge of West Gallatin river below Spanish creek, Mont., 1891-'92.

increased, rendering it possible to cover at least 100,000 acres, an amount which would probably embrace the greater part of the irrigable land along the stream.

The Gallatin valley, as well as the great part of the catchment area of the river, is included within Gallatin county, Montana, the lines of this county extending in a westerly direction to the Jefferson river and thus including the valleys at the mouth of Madison river and Willow creek. The statistics of the Eleventh census show that in this county there were 434 irrigated farms, upon which 46,901 acres of crops were raised, the average size of the irrigated holding being thus 108 acres. These farms were mainly along the eastern edge of the Gallatin valley in the vicinity of Bozeman and northwesterly from this locality along the foothills.

The altitude of Gallatin valley may be taken in round numbers as from 4,000 to 5,000 feet above sea level. At Bozeman, on its eastern side, the railroad track is at an elevation of 4,754 feet, while at Gallatin, at the lower end of the valley near the Missouri river, the elevation of the track is 4,032 feet. The fall is thus sufficiently great at all points to render possible the diversion of water from the streams upon nearly all of the bench lands, so that there are few limitations of this kind to the development of irrigation systems.

The water from the small streams which make up the East Gallatin has been appropriated and utilized by farmers, the only exception being in the case of waters during the spring floods. Toward the end of summer the streams become very small and there is not a sufficient supply to fill the demands made upon them. During the drought of 1889 and 1890 there was not sufficient water to irrigate all of the land under cultivation, and the necessity of storing some of the surplus water of spring became more than ever apparent. One or two enterprises of this character have been begun, but as yet have not come into active operation. There have been many complaints of injustice on the part of various individuals claiming water from the small streams, some of the older settlers asserting that they have been deprived of what was rightfully theirs, and, on the other hand, many of the later comers assert that the waters have not been fairly divided.

The principal irrigating streams, taken in order from the West Gallatin easterly around the valley, are given below, together with the average amount of water flowing during the irrigating season as estimated by a resident of Bozeman:

	Second-feet.		Second-feet.
Wilson creek	16	Bridger creek	30
Bear creek	20	Little Cottonwood creek	12
Cottonwood creek	30	Spring creek	20
Middle creek	50	Reese creek	20
Bozeman creek	24	Dry creek	16
Reservation creek	24		

Bozeman, Reservation, and Bridger creeks unite to form the East Gallatin river. The streams below this, namely, Little Cottonwood, Spring, Reese, and Dry, seldom reach the river except during the spring floods. The water supply from the streams named above, together with that taken from the West Gallatin river, aggregates 522 second-feet, assuming that the amount contributed by the canals from this latter river is as follows: West Gallatin and Bozeman canal, 100 second-feet; Excelsior canal, 100 second-feet, and Middle Creek ditch, 60 second-feet.

Near the edges of the valley, among the foothills, a few 'crops can occasionally be raised without irrigation. For example, winter wheat in years of abundant snowfall yields largely. Also on the low grounds along the river, where the fall is slight, are areas where irrigation is not essential, but these are comparatively small, and it may be said

U.S.GEOLOGICAL SURVEY.

114°

that the value of the lands of the valley rests immediately upon the amount of water supply and the thoroughness with which this is utilized.

While there has been a considerable development of agriculture by means of the waters of the smaller streams, the greatest increase of area tilled since the census year comes through the construction and extension of a few large canals taking water from the West Gallatin river. These head in or near the mouth of the canyon and take the water out upon both sides of the river, covering on the west side at least a large portion of the bench lands. There are two canals on the east side, the Bozeman and West Gallatin canal and the Excelsior, these running toward the northeast in the direction of Bozeman and approximately parallel to each other. The latter was built by an association of farmers in the attempt to secure water at less rates than those offered by the first-named company.

The canal of the West Gallatin Irrigation Company heads on the west side of the river a little over 3 miles above Salesville, and after following the stream for several miles turns off to the west, passing through a ridge or spur by means of a tunnel and then out upon the bench lands lying between the Gallatin and Madison rivers. The surface is greatly eroded by small streams which flow in spring from the mountains, and many of these gulches are crossed by flumes. The total length of this canal as completed during 1891 was 23 miles, and the average bottom width 14 feet. It can be made to cover approximately 60,000 acres, the greater part if not all of which is arable.

Besides the three large canals mentioned above there are many ditches taking water from both sides of the stream and carrying it out upon the land in the lower end of the valley and over toward Three Forks. Some of the best farms, if not the finest in the whole state, are in this vicinity, and, as shown by the irrigators, the crops which have been produced can not be excelled by any in Montana for quantity as well as quality.

Settlement began in the Gallatin valley, according to statement of a correspondent, in 1863, crops of grain and vegetables being raised in the following year. Since that time there has been a steady increase year by year in the acreage under cultivation by irrigation, so that now a great part of the valley is covered by a network of ditches. Irrigation is regarded by all as indispensable, although as previously stated, there are a few farms lying near the mountains where it is apparent that the late spring and early summer rains fall more copiously and later in the season than they do upon the lower lands, and it is here that the winter wheat can be relied upon with a reasonable degree of confidence to produce a remunerative crop. By irrigation, however, the yield could be greatly increased, and it is only because this is impracticable that the so-called dry farming is attempted.

On the lower, moist grounds along the rivers or near the swamps in the valley large crops have been raised from the time of the settlement of the valley without the soil apparently losing its fertility, but, unfortunately, the alkaline salts tend to develop in such localities, destroying the value of the land unless great care is used to neutralize the effect of these minerals. It is stated that land in this valley has been producing wheat, oats, and barley for over twenty years without signs of deterioration, and now produces from 35 to 45 bushels of wheat per acre without artificial fertilizers.

Until the drought of 1889 the farmers deemed it sufficient to provide irrigation for only a small portion of their farms, relying upon seepage to furnish sufficient moisture for other parts. The experience of that year, however, showed the necessity of having a reserve supply of water and of providing ditches to use in time of unusual drought. Without an ample supply and a thorough system of distributing the amount available irrigation, in the words of one who has had experience, "becomes a constant source of trouble and worry. There is more litigation and bad feeling among farmers over water rights and the use of water than in all other affairs combined."

MADISON RIVER.

The Madison river rises in the Yellowstone National park southeast of the head waters of the West Gallatin, a great part of the water coming from the hot springs and geysers of Firehole river and other streams in the park. It flows in a general westerly and northwesterly direction for about 40 miles through canyons, then turns toward the north, and soon after enters Madison valley, a long narrow opening bounded at both ends by canyons through which the river flows. The catchment area of this stream above Madison valley is in most respects similar to that of the West Gallatin, with the possible exception that the slopes may be a trifle less steep and the water delivered with a little less rapidity to the stream.

Below Madison valley the river continues in the lower canyon for over 10 miles before the walls again fall back. The gauging station of the Geological Survey is in this canyon at a point a short distance below the mouth of Hot Spring creek. The measurements obtained at this place represent therefore the amount of water flowing out of Madison valley, a comparatively small quantity being added during the passage of the river through the canyon.

Madison valley lies at a general altitude of from 4,800 to 5,000 feet. It is over 30 miles in length from north to south, and upwards of 8 miles in width at about its center. There is no railroad in the valley, the only means of transportation being by wagon road across the mountains. In spite of this fact, however, agriculture has developed to a comparatively large extent owing to the ready market for supplies at mining towns in that part of the state.

DISCHARGE OF MADISON RIVER.

The water used for irrigation in Madison valley is taken almost exclusively from the creeks which come from the mountains on both sides. These on the east rise to heights of over 10,000 feet, and the streams draining their slopes carry a considerable amount of water throughout the year. The main river, traversing the valley from south to north, is little used on account of the fact that small ditches can be built from the side streams to cover the arable lands at far less expense and by the exercise of less skill than from the river.

As in the case of the other valleys of Montana, the droughts of 1889 and 1890 impressed upon the farmers the fact that irrigation works must be so planned and constructed that they will receive an ample supply under unusual circumstances. In these years far more water than usual was required, and in 1890 much of the land had to be irrigated in order to plow it, or to enable the crops to start. In ordinary seasons no irrigation is necessary in this valley for the first crop of lucern, and it is customary to give only one watering to small grain. In these latter years of drought there was no decided loss of crops, but the yield was not as large as usual owing to the scarcity of water at critical times.

This valley is in the east end of Madison county, which extends from the summits of Madison range westerly to Jefferson river. The county thus includes several localities besides Madison valley in which irrigation is practiced. According to the census the total number of irrigators in the county was 345 and the acreage of crop irrigated 36,819, giving an average of 107 acres per farm. It is evident from the average size of the crop areas that the methods of applying water must be comparatively crude and that it is used with little care and personal attention. The irrigating ditches are small and are owned usually by a few farmers, there being but one or two systems of notable size.

It is probable that the Madison river can be diverted by means of large canals, one on each side of the valley, and by this means bring under irrigation all of the lowland and even a portion of the benches, and that by a well planned system the higher benches can be cultivated by means of the water from the side streams. It will be necessary, however, to make careful surveys before the feasibility of such projects can be determined. In the north end of the valley near Meadow creek is a large area of arable land, the water supply for which is at present insufficient. This can undoubtedly be irrigated, however, in part at least by the construction of storage reservoirs on Meadow creek, as, for example, at North Meadow creek lake, where, it is stated, the water can readily be held. At present the farmers in this locality state that owing to scarcity of water they can not raise sufficient hay to carry the stock through the winter, and that there are heavy losses in consequence.

The gauging station of the Geological Survey, as noted in the second annual report, is below the mouth of Hot Spring creek, 4 miles from the town of Red Bluff, at Hayward bridge.[1] The results of the computations of discharge are shown in Fig. 54, which gives the daily discharge for 1891 and for the first half of 1892. This diagram should be compared with that on Pl. LXI, in the Twelfth Annual Report,[2] where is given diagrammatically the quantity of water in the river in 1890 and during the early months of 1891. Reference should also be made to the table of mean monthly and annual discharge on page 92 of the present report.

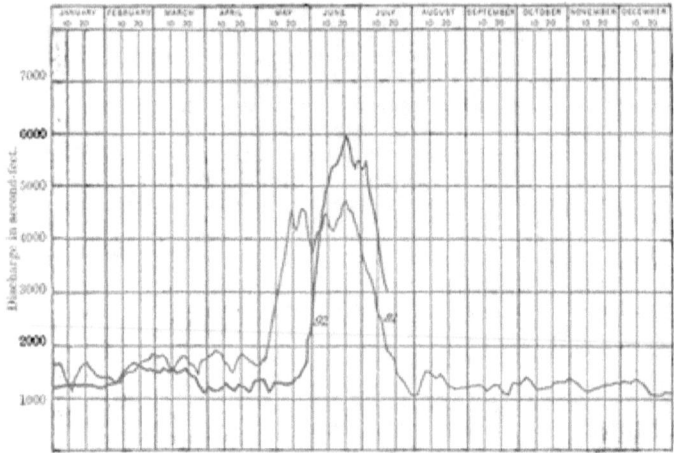

Fig. 54.—Diagram of daily discharge of Madison river near Red Bluff, Mont., 1891 and 1892.

About 6 miles below the gauging station the Madison river crosses the county line and enters Gallatin county, and a short distance beyond this point the valley widens, opening out into the western prolongation of Gallatin valley. Comparatively little irrigation is carried on along the river on account of the difficulty and expense of diverting water. From the topography of the country, however, it would appear that large canals can be built to carry water upon the bench lands upon each side. The practicability of such schemes can only be determined by survey. The amount of water available, as shown by the stream measurements, is large, the average for three years being over 1,900 second-feet. This, at a water duty of 100 acres to the second-foot, would irrigate 190,000 acres, an amount far greater than can probably be covered by canals. Thus the water supply along the Madison river if properly utilized will probably be far in excess of the demands made upon it.

---

[1] See U. S. Geol. Survey, Eleventh Ann. Rept., 1889-90, pt. 2, p. 40.
[2] U. S. Geol. Survey, Twelfth Ann. Rept., pt. 2, Irrigation, p. 230.

HEADWATERS OF JEFFERSON RIVER. 49

The bench land on the west side of the Madison river contains a body of arable land probably as good as any in the state. This land extends from Three Forks up the Madison river for 10 or 12 miles and west to Willow creek, a distance of nearly 8 miles. Little, if any, of this land is under cultivation, on account of the expense of constructing a canal. One-half of the land to be benefited is reported to belong to the Northern Pacific railroad, which owns alternate sections. At present there are only a few hay ranches along the stream, the owners being engaged in stock-raising. Wherever the ground is sufficiently moist a little hay is cut without irrigation, but away from the flood plains of the rivers nothing can be raised at present. The soil, however, is very rich, and although it now produces merely a stunted growth of bunchgrass, by irrigation upwards of 40 bushels of wheat and 60 of oats per acre can be raised.

JEFFERSON RIVER.

The drainage basin of the Jefferson lies west of that of the Madison and includes the area surrounded on the south and west by the great bend or loop in the continental divide or watershed. The drainage area of this stream is over four times as great as that of the Madison, but, in spite of this fact, the mean annual discharge of the stream is probably not as great, owing to the difference in character of topography and the lower elevation. The main stream is formed by the union of Bighole river, coming in from the west, and the Beaverhead from the south. From this point the river flows in a general northeasterly course for a distance of 60 miles to its junction with the Madison and Gallatin, forming the Missouri river.

Redrock creek, the head waters of Beaverhead river, rises in the mountains south of Madison valley and flows west, parallel to the continental divide, through a broad open valley, in which are numerous small lakes and marshes, furnishing excellent pasturage. This is known as Centennial valley. It is about 40 miles long and from 2 to 3 miles in width, and lies at an elevation of about 6,000 feet. Redrock creek, after flowing beyond the line between Madison and Beaverhead counties, turns toward the north and flows through an open though broken country, suitable principally for grazing. The bed of the stream frequently becomes nearly dry at various points in Beaverhead county during the latter part of summer, and it will be necessary to store some of the water in order to increase the acreage of irrigated crops.

A gauging station was established on April 9, 1890, at Redrock, a short distance above the mouth of Horse Prairie creek, and measurements were continued until October. The average discharge for the year is estimated to have been 148 second-feet. The daily discharge of Redrock creek for the time during which observations were made is shown in the twelfth annual report, part 2, Pl. LX, in connection with the diagram for the West Gallatin river. The drainage area is 1,330

13 GEOL., PT. III——4

square miles, and this amount of water would cover this area to a depth of 1½ inches. The mean annual run-off from this catchment area was a little over 0.1 of a second-foot per square mile. A measurement was made of Redrock creek at Alderdice, about 20 miles above Redrock, the discharge on September 6, 1890, being 10 second-feet.

Below Redrock station several important tributaries enter the stream, the principal of those from the west being Horse Prairie, Grasshopper, and Rattlesnake creeks, and from the east Blacktail Deer creek. The latter stream was measured on September 4, 1889, at Poindexter, the discharge being only 10 second-feet from a drainage area of 300 square miles. This amount may be considered as the waste or seepage water from the ditches above.

The Beaverhead river, formed by the union of the creeks named above, flows toward the northeast through an open country having an elevation of from 4,800 to 5,400 feet, the valley lands extending on each side up tributary streams. The water supply, especially in summer, is very scanty on account of the fact that the head waters of these streams are among comparatively low, broad mountains, from which the rain and snow water is not discharged with rapidity. In the higher valleys the various forage plants, with the exception of alfalfa, are raised, and also wheat, oats, and barley, the climate being in general too cold for corn and many of the common fruits.

In consequence of the scanty supply of water and the lack of efficient regulations governing the distribution of it, controversies are constantly arising concerning the use of the water, and these lead to almost endless litigation. It is impossible for the agricultural resources to be developed until the water supply is increased by storage and until a thorough system of water control is inaugurated, so that the irrigator may be reasonably sure of receiving a fair proportion of water each year.

In many of the upper valleys, as, for example, on Grasshopper creek, the settlers for nearly thirty years have raised nothing but hay along creek bottoms. They have not produced even the common garden vegetables, but many of them are convinced that if the lands were thoroughly cultivated and the water not allowed to run to waste, but stored and held for use during the summer, the production per acre could be increased threefold, and the water could be made to cover many times as much land as it does at present. It is stated that under present methods the full limit of farming has been reached, and that when a ranch is taken higher up on the river and irrigated some person further down the stream must stop farming for lack of water. One farmer states that when he bought his land he had an abundant supply, but as other persons brought under cultivation land higher and higher up on the river and its tributaries, he, with others, began to lose the usual supply, and as a result all parties are engaged in lawsuits.

Near Dillon a deep well has been drilled to a depth of 450 feet, at a cost of about $5,000, in the hopes of obtaining artesian water. There is especial need here for water for the farms already under cultivation, not to mention the thousands of acres that might be cultivated if water could be had. The farmers, as a rule, see the imperfection of the present methods of irrigation, but are unable to unite upon any practicable plan to remedy matters. The first settlers claim most, if not all, of the water during dry seasons, and the later comers do not see why they are not entitled to as much water as the others.

The Bighole, or, as it was formerly known, Wisdom river, rises in the mountain ranges northwest of the headwaters of Beaverhead river. It flows northerly through broad, open valleys, then turns to the east and southeast, describing roughly a half circle in a general way parallel to that formed by the continental divide. It is probable that this river carries a larger amount of water than does the Beaverhead, but, unfortunately, few measurements have been made. On September 8, 1889, the Bighole, as measured at Melrose, was discharging only 60 second-feet from a drainage area of 2,335 square miles. At about the same time, viz, September 9, the Beaverhead, at Dillon, **where the drainage area is** approximately 4,000 square miles, was discharging 75 second-feet.

When the upper valleys along this stream were first settled it was found that good hay grew in abundance along the river and on the small creek bottoms that were overflowed in spring and early summer. These lands were rapidly taken up, and for many years the inhabitants were **successful in** raising sufficient hay for their **cattle without irrigation.** In 1889, however, there was almost **complete failure of crops on** such land, but those persons who had taken water out upon the bench or high lands had a fairly good crop.

A **short distance** above the junction of the Beaverhead and Bighole rivers **Ruby** creek enters from the southeast, bringing water from the Jefferson range, Ruby range, and other mountains, the drainage basin of this river being included within Madison county. This **stream is** reported to flow continuously throughout the year, and **the ditches** depending upon it usually receive **an amount** of water sufficient for ordinary needs. In the case of many of the tributaries, however, the supply is less abundant, some of them becoming dry during summer. A measurement of Ruby creek was made at Laurin on September 4, 1889, and the discharge was found to be 90 second-feet from a drainage area of approximately 710 square miles.

There is complaint that the ditches are **too small and that the loss by** evaporation and seepage is enormous; also, **that the construction has been so poor that the** annual expense of maintenance is a serious matter to the irrigator. There **is a great need not only here, but elsewhere in the basin, of storage reservoirs near the head** of the river, and of **more thorough systems of employing** the water already available. It is **stated that there is great wastage from lack of** definite rules regarding the use of the water, some persons allowing it to run where it does no good, or neglecting to employ it properly in spring and fall. The ground also is not always properly prepared, and the losses through ignorance and carelessness are often greater than those through scarcity of supply.

Along the lower part of the Beaverhead many farms depend upon seepage and overflow, the only crop raised being hay. The cultivated lands lie higher and must be irrigated by means of ditches before anything can be produced, the only exception being in the case of certain soils which, in an unusually rainy season, retain sufficient moisture to support an inferior growth. In 1890, as well as in 1889, the Beaverhead was dry in certain places and it is probable that this condition of things will occur again and again, since more land is being brought under cultivation on the tributaries each year. The only apparent relief is from storage reservoirs. In a few instances alkali is reported to have developed on some of the lower lands to an extent sufficient to kill grass and other plants, resulting in partial or complete abandonment of these spots.

Below the junction of the Beaverhead and Bighole rivers the Jefferson receives a number of tributaries, the principal of these from the north being Pipestone, Whitetail Deer, and North Boulder creeks, these being in Jefferson county, and from the south Coal, Bell, South Boulder, and Willow creeks, these coming from the Jefferson range.

On North Boulder creek, as on many of the other streams, there is great scarcity of water, and as the settlers bring more and more land under cultivation the demand steadily increases. In this part of the state examples are furnished of the changes in industry, the first settlers being attracted by mining, and then to some extent taking up stock-raising. After awhile the stock ranges become overstocked, and during the dry seasons the grass has been almost destroyed. As a consequence the settlers have turned their attention more and more to agriculture, and the strife for water has become severe. It is asserted that there is not sufficient water along North Boulder creek for one acre out of ten of the tillable lands unless some is saved by storage. In the dry seasons of 1889 and 1890 this creek and the Little Boulder were very low, and even dry in places, and the floods, which generally wet the bottom lands in April and May, were too small to be of much benefit.

The drainage basin of Jefferson river includes all of Beaverhead county, the southern part of Silverbow county, the western part of Madison and the south end of Jefferson county. According to the census there were in Beaverhead county 294 irrigators and a total crop area of 42,606 acres irrigated, the average size of farm being 145 acres. In Silverbow county there were 75 irrigators and 5,968 acres irrigated, most of this undoubtedly being along the Bighole river or its tributaries. In Jefferson and Madison counties the acreage irrigated, as previously stated, lies partly in other basins.

MISSOURI VALLEY.

This name is commonly applied to the long, narrow valley lying for the most part on the east side of the Missouri river southeast of Helena. The river below Three Forks continues northerly for about 20 miles, principally in a gorge or canyon. At Toston the valley begins to widen, the river keeping its course near the hills on the western side, leaving broad bench and low lands on the east. The valley terminates near Canyon Ferry, a point 18 miles from Helena in a direction a little north of east. A large number of streams rising in the Belt mountains enter this valley from the east, furnishing a well distributed though small water supply.

Irrigation in the Missouri valley is carried on mainly by means of water from the tributaries, the water of the main river being used to a very small extent, if at all. This is due to the fact that ditches can be diverted from the side streams with far greater ease than from the river on account of their decided fall and the elevation of their beds relative to the lands to be irrigated. The water in these streams decreases rapidly in July and many of them become dry later in the season. In 1889 it is reported that not to exceed one-fourth of a crop was raised in the valley, and in many instances there was an entire failure owing to scarcity of water. In the following year the condition of affairs was a little better, but some farmers failed to obtain fair returns.

The quantity of water in the streams varies greatly with the character of the weather during the winter season. If the fall is dry and there is a large amount of snow during winter a large part of this saturates the ground, but, on the other hand, if the ground is frozen before snow comes it often melts and runs away without being of benefit. The farmers have become accustomed to estimating the probable amount of water available during the succeeding season and as far as possible regulate their crops in accordance with the probabilities.

The great need of this valley is of a large canal taking water from the Missouri river and bringing it out at an elevation sufficient to cover the thousands of acres of excellent land. Whether this is practicable can be determined only by thorough examination of the route of such a canal.[1] If this could be done then the water of the side streams could be used upon bench lands above the reach of the canal. As regards water supply there can be no question, for the amount in the river, as shown by measurements, is ample for all demands of this kind.

The amount of water in the Missouri river at the head of the valley is practically the same as that at the junction of the Gallatin, Madison, and Jefferson, since only a few small streams enter between these two places. The measurements of flowing water made in this part of the

---

[1] Eleventh Ann. Rept. U. S. Geol. Survey, pt. 2, Irrigation, p. 114.

river have been previously mentioned on p. 39. The details of those made at Toston from April 8 to July 26, 1890, are given on page 42 of the second annual report.[1] According to these measurements the discharge at that time varied from 3,697 second-feet to 14,440. The measurements made by T. P. Roberts in 1872 are mentioned on p. 236 of the third annual report,[2] the result obtained by him in the latter part of July being 8,538 second-feet. On July 28, 1890, the discharge, as measured by the Missouri River Commission, was 2,863 second-feet, and on August 6, 1890, 2,640 second-feet.

Besides the computations of discharge made for localities above the valley, others, as given on p. 39, were made for stations at the lower end of the valley, where the river again enters the canyons, viz, at Canyon Ferry, Stubbs Ferry, and localities in that vicinity. A comparison of the results obtained at these places, together with those from the gauging station at Craig, shows that at the time of greatest drought the river rarely falls below 2,000 second-feet, so that at all times there will be an ample supply in the river for use upon the irrigable lands. As previously stated, a permanent station has been established at Townsend by the Missouri River Commission, where records of the fluctuations of the height of the stream are being kept.

The quantity of water delivered by the streams coming from the Big Belt mountains is not known, but there is unquestionably an amount sufficiently large to fill during the spring numerous reservoirs among the foothills. By saving the surplus water in this way a larger acreage could be brought under cultivation in the Missouri valley, and it is possible that the greater part of the land could in time be irrigated should a large canal from the Missouri river prove impracticable. On the other hand, even with a canal of this character there would still remain elevated tracts on the bench lands to be supplied with water from storage.

The eastern side of Missouri valley is in the western end of Meagher county, the river forming the county line, while the land on the opposite bank of the stream is in Jefferson county. In this latter locality most of the farmers depend for irrigation mainly upon water from the Missouri river, taking it out during flood time. When the stream falls they can no longer bring the water out upon their ground and in summer the crops often are very scanty on account of the lack of moisture. The streams from the Jefferson range are less in number and carry a smaller amount of water than is the case of those from the Belt mountains in the east.

PRICKLY PEAR VALLEY.

Prickly Pear valley is northwest of Missouri valley, lying on the west side of the Missouri river and beginning nearly opposite the lower end of this latter valley. The Jefferson mountains are on the south and

---
[1] U. S. Geol. Survey, Eleventh Ann. Rept., pt. ii, Irrigation, p. 42.
[2] Twelfth Ann. Rept. U. S. Geol. Survey, pt. 2. Irrigation. p. 236.

the continental divide with its spurs on the west and north. The city of Helena, the capital of Montana, is on the southwestern edge of the open land. The elevation of the valley is from 3,800 to 4,200 feet, the railroad at the city of Helena being 3,932 feet above sea level. The valley is nearly 12 miles wide and 20 miles long, but, although comparatively thickly settled, the water supply is deficient. Wherever water can be obtained, however, the land is thoroughly cultivated.

In the Prickly Pear valley there are thousands of acres of arable land which by irrigation would produce heavy crops. Unfortunately the Missouri river is at an elevation too low to be brought out upon any of this land, for, as previously stated, the elevation of low water at Toston is 3,879 feet and at Craig, 3,629. The only way of increasing the water supply, therefore, is by storing the spring floods. Occasionally there have been seasons in which there was sufficient rainfall to produce a good crop anywhere in the valley, but from 1888 to 1890 the precipitation has either been too small, or has come at times when it was of little benefit to agriculture, and it is evident that no dependence can be placed upon the success of farming without irrigation.

The facilities for storing water are reported to be excellent, as there are many localities where water, in small quantities at least, could be held for use during the dry season. The matter has been frequently discussed by the irrigators, but comparatively little work has been done toward making these resources available. Attempts have been made to obtain water by deep wells, one being drilled at Helena to a depth of 1,000 feet. Water was found at 160 feet, but it did not rise to the surface. Another well has been drilled to a depth of 521 feet, and this and other shallower wells are pumped by windmills, each furnishing water for about an acre of ground.

In some portions of the valley are a few swamps and hay lands kept moist by springs or seepage, but in other parts there has been a succession of losses of crops owing to deficiency of water. In the southern part of the valley the irrigators depend upon water from Prickley Pear creek, which flows north from the Jefferson range. A few own private ditches, while others have joined in forming companies in order to build canals and ditches. There has been more or less contention over the division of water. In a few instances it is stated that prior locators whose rights have been confirmed by decisions of court find it more profitable to sell the water to more unfortunate irrigators than to attempt to use it themselves.

DEARBORN AND SUN RIVERS.

The Dearborn and Sun rivers rise in the main range of the Rocky mountains and flow easterly to the Missouri, the Dearborn entering at a point about 50 miles north of Helena and the Sun river at an equal distance further down the river. A large number of creeks flow into the stream between these points, but they are of comparatively little importance in irrigation. On the Dearborn river are several large irrigating canals, the one on the north fork being perhaps the most extensive in the state. There is no continuous record of the amount of water in this stream, the only measurements known being those made at Dearborn on August 9, 1889, the discharge being 47 second-feet, and on April 15, 1890, 37 second-feet. The drainage area at this point is about 350 square miles.

In this vicinity are large areas of table or bench land along the Missouri river and extending back to the mountains. The soil on these lands would be very productive if an ample supply of water could be secured. The Missouri river, however, is, as in the case of Prickly Pear valley, at too low an elevation to furnish the needed supply. In times of drought the small streams become dry often at points above the heads of the farmers' ditches. Even the comparatively large streams, as the Dearborn and Sun, contract to such an extent that it becomes a matter of conjecture as to where the water for the large canals is to come from.

Along the beds of the small dry creeks a number of storage reservoirs have been built by ranchmen, who find that in this way they can save enough water to bring under irrigation patches of forage crop of considerable size. This method of saving water is being gradually extended, although the capital invested in such works is small on account of the limited means of the owners. Water is always plentiful in the spring, and if advantage is taken of this fact at the proper time these small ponds can be filled.

The Sun river has been described with considerable detail in the second annual report,[1] where is given a map of the basin, showing the reservoirs and canal lines surveyed by H. M. Wilson. The details of the work are given on page 121 of this volume. The discharge of the Sun river is shown graphically on Plate LXIII of the third annual report,[2] and the maximum, minimum, and mean discharges by months are given in the table on page 347 of the same volume. By reference to this table it will be seen that the discharge for 1890 ranged from 160 second-feet up to 4,085 second-feet. The average for the year was 715 second-feet, this amount of water coming from a drainage area of about 1,175 square miles. The possible utilization of this water out upon the great plains on both sides of the Sun river, both in Lewis and Clarke and Choteau counties, and in Cascade county, above Great Falls, has been discussed by Mr. Wilson in other reports.

The irrigators depending for water upon the smaller streams in this part of the country state that the water supply is barely sufficient for present demands, and that there are large tracts of land on every side now valueless for lack of water. Much of this can be irrigated only by storing the spring floods, but, unfortunately, the farmers do not have

---

[1] Eleventh Ann. Rept. U. S. Geol. Survey, pt. II, Irrigation, pages 120 to 133.
[2] Twelfth Ann. Rept. U. S. Geol. Survey, pt. II, Irrigation, p. 284.

sufficient capital to build the small reservoirs. The demand for water is increasing with great rapidity since the ranges upon which the cattle have been accustomed to feed are being fenced and the stockmen are compelled to raise more and more feed for their cattle.

The drainage basin of the Dearborn river, the south part of that of the Sun river, and the Prickly Pear valley are principally in Lewis and Clarke county, in which area, according to the last census, there were 231 irrigators, and a total of 15,441 acres irrigated from which crops were obtained. The average size of the area irrigated by each person was thus 67 acres, an amount considerably less than the average for the state, but still large when compared with the carefully cultivated areas of Utah and of adjoining states.

CHESTNUT VALLEY AND SMITH RIVER.

Chestnut valley is the term applied to the open land along the Missouri river above Great Falls and north of the Big Belt mountains. Smith river, which drains the country between the Big and Little Belt mountains, enters the Missouri river near the lower end of this valley. A large proportion of the lower land of this area can be irrigated by means of a canal from the Missouri. One canal has already been built, but owing to improper plan or construction a sufficient supply of water could not be turned into it during the drought of 1889 and succeeding years.

The quantity of water in the river available for irrigation is very large, as shown by measurements made at various points referred to on the preceding pages. The daily discharge at Craig, a point north of Helena and above the mouth of the Dearborn river, is shown in Fig. 55. The discharge in 1891, as indicated by the light line, was considerably less than in 1892. This figure should be compared with Pl. LXII of the Twelfth Annual Report,[1] which also gives diagrammatically the discharge during the early part of 1891, together with the quantities for 1890 and for the latter part of 1889. The increased discharge of 1892 over that for 1890 and 1891 is especially noticeable.

There is a large amount of bottom land along the Missouri river usually overflowed each year in the month of June and producing heavy crops of wild hay. Occasionally, however, in years of drought there is no overflow and little hay can be cut. The construction of canals built in such manner as to insure a permanent supply of water for the valley must necessarily involve large expenditures, but the certainty of securing water offers inducements toward investment of this character. In this part of the state there have been a number of large canals built at heavy expense, but which have been to a greater or less degree failures on account of errors of judgment as to the quantity of water available or through poor engineering in locating the line of canal.

---

[1] U. S. Geol. Survey, Twelfth Ann. Rept., pt. II, Irrigation, p. 282.

It is stated that the charge for water from the large canal in Chestnut valley is $2 per miner's inch a season, and that one-half an inch to the acre is sufficient, but in dry seasons the farmers claim that they can not succeed in raising good crops with this amount of water. Occasionally fair crops can be raised without irrigation, but with a thorough system every acre of this beautiful valley could be made to produce large crops every year.

The headwaters of Smith river are in Meagher county, while the lower part, near Chestnut valley, is in Cascade county. As in the case of nearly all streams which flow from one county to another, there is

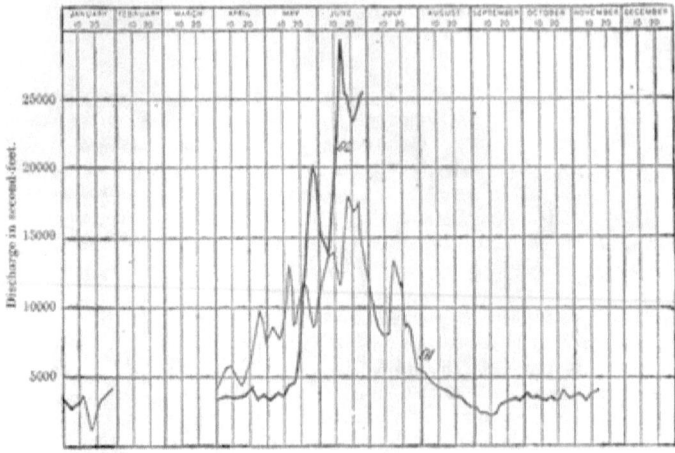

FIG. 55.—Diagram of daily discharge of Missouri river at Craig, Montana, for 1891 and 1892.

more or less friction among the irrigators of each locality regarding the distribution of the water during the summer. In the upper valleys, where the agricultural areas are small, the water supply is comparatively abundant and is used freely and even wastefully on hay lands. Further down the amount of water available steadily diminishes until the point is finally reached where there is not sufficient for the land usually cultivated.

On the headwaters of the south fork of Smith river from 15 to 20 miles southerly from White Sulphur springs a number of reservoirs have been examined by the Geological Survey and reported for segregation as described on pages 137 et seq., of the third annual report. At White Sulphur springs the valley has an elevation of about 5,000 feet, and the Smith river is usually considered as a small sized creek. All of the ditches in this vicinity are owned by individuals who take as much water from the streams as they need. Occasionally, however, when there is an unusual drought there is even at this point considerable litigation concerning the distribution of this water. Probably more land could be brought under cultivation if storage reservoirs were constructed in the localities favorable for such work.

In the eastern end of Cascade county near the lower part of Smith river valley the country is in general broken, and the only part suitable for cultivation is that along small, narrow bottoms in the coulees which lead down from the mountains to some water course. In some of these coulees, or draws as they are locally called, there are small streams of water from springs which flow even during the dry season. This water is used by each settler in irrigating a few acres of grain or a garden, but there are few ditches of notable size. There has been little, if any, effort made to provide water storage.

East of Smith river are a number of streams deriving their water from the northern end of the Little Belt mountains or from the Highwood mountains which occupy an almost isolated position to the north of these. A few ditches have been taken out of Little Belt creek, Otter creek and Big Belt creek, but these were of comparatively little use during times of severe drought. In fact, as stated by one of the irrigators, when there is sufficient water to fill the ditches no irrigation is needed and they are practically useless. On the other hand, when the drought is unusually severe the only possible means of irrigation would be by water held in reservoirs near the Highwood mountains.

TETON AND MARIAS RIVERS.

The Teton and Marias rivers rise in the Rocky mountains in the northwestern corner of the Missouri basin and flow in an easterly direction through a region of elevated plains and prairies, finally joining the Missouri river. The general altitude of this country is from 3,000 to 4,000 feet, towards the mountains the plains rising by gentle terraces to elevations of about 5,000 feet. This, as shown on Pl. CVIII, is a broad grazing country, cattle finding an ample supply of grass, especially during years of ordinary rainfall. There are very few cultivated farms, and these are found along the streams where water can be obtained.

On these plains crops can occasionally be raised without irrigation, but there is by no means certainty of success in any year. There are few settlements in this part of Montana, the towns being mainly along the Missouri river. Irrigation is practiced principally near the headwaters of the Teton river, and also on the Marias to a small extent. At various times large irrigating systems have been proposed to take water from these streams out upon the almost limitless plains lying in all directions. On the Blackfeet agency a small ditch has been built and the ground under it cultivated. The Indians attempted to raise crops without irrigation, but during 1889 and 1890 these were a failure.

Along Dupuyer creek, the most southerly of the upper tributaries of the Marias, ditches have been taken out by ranchmen either for the purpose of making hay from the wild prairie grass or for the cultivation of crops. The fall of the land affords means for the easy and rapid construction of ditches and the water of the creek is all taken or claimed, except the flood waters of spring. The surroundings are reported to be very favorable for the construction of reservoirs, but the cost is beyond the means of individuals. The losses for want of water in 1889 in the valley of the Dupuyer alone are stated to have been nearly $40,000. The land is very fertile and produces remarkable quantities of wheat, oats, barley and potatoes.

All along the foot of the Rocky mountains in this part of the basin of the Missouri river are small streams which can be utilized for irrigation, covering the level land in their immediate vicinity. Further out on the plains, however, where the soil is of great fertility, the water supply is very scanty and can only be increased by the most careful system of storage. It is not probable that more than a small percentage of this vast area can ever be cultivated by means of irrigation, and it must remain useful only as pasturage. There are many natural basins into which water from melting snow could be conducted and held for use upon lower grounds in July and August. At present most of this land belongs to the government and affords free pasturage, so that there is little necessity of raising forage plants.

The valley of the Teton is in places 3 miles wide and is at least 70 miles long. Stock-raising is the principal industry, for, since the only railroad is along the Missouri river, there are no facilities for transporting products. It has not been found profitable to raise grain, but the land is rich and with irrigation will produce large crops. On August 7, 1889, the Teton at Choteau was discharging 26 second-feet.

JUDITH AND MUSSELSHELL RIVERS.

The Judith and Musselshell rivers receive the greater part of the drainage of the Missouri basin east of the Little Belt mountains and south of the main river. The headwaters of the Musselshell are south of those of the Judith, this stream flowing in an easterly direction for over 100 miles out upon the Great Plain region before turning north to join the Missouri. Both of these streams receive water from broad basins partially encircled by mountains rising to heights of from 6,000 to 9,000 feet. The general elevation of these upper valleys is a little over 4,000 feet. They are comparatively well watered, many streams issuing from the mountains at short intervals. As a consequence there are a great many small ditches owned by individuals and few, if any, systems of irrigation owned by corporations.

In the Judith basin there is occasionally a year during which a paying crop can be raised without irrigation by the careful cultivation of certain lands, but there is seldom a time in which the crops would not be better by the employment of water. It is stated that 1887 was the wettest year known, and that in 1888 there was ample rain until the 1st of July. In both of these years, good crops were raised in the valley without the use of water, but in 1889 and 1890, the snows in the mountains were very light and the rainfall so deficient that as a consequence most of the crops failed even where settlers were prepared to irrigate, the streams not furnishing sufficient water. A number of storage sites have beeen selected by this survey, and by the construction of reservoirs in these or other favorable localities the cultivated area could be greatly extended.

Judith valley was settled within a comparatively few years, the first ditch being taken out of the Judith river in 1880. As is usually the case, the majority of farmers were poor and made their ditches at as little expense as possible. As a consequence many of these are inefficient and there is considerable waste of water. The claim is made by the farmers that better ditches are needed, as well as laws to regulate the use of water, especially during the time of drought, which begins in the latter part of July. The greater part of the drainage basin of the Judith and Musselshell rivers is included within Fergus county, where, according to the last census, there were 251 irrigators, having a total of 30,401 acres of crops under irrigation. The average size of crop area per individual, viz, 121 acres, shows that most of this must have been devoted to raising hay.

The headwaters of Musselshell river are on the south side of the Little Belt mountains, many streams coming from the Elk mountains on the west and the Crazy mountains on the south. The principal areas irrigated are in the vicinity of Martindale. In this vicinity each farm or ranch as a rule has a ditch of its own, and the bottom lands along the streams are alone watered, these being but a small fraction of the arable land which could be brought under irrigation if reservoirs were constructed on the small tributaries. On each of the small streams there are usually several persons claiming the water which is sufficient to supply only one farm. The bench land, which now furnishes scanty feed to cattle, would with irrigation produce good grain or pasturage for large herds. At the head of many of these creeks or along their course reservoir sites have been segregated.

A few measurements of streams have been made in this vicinity, and it was found that on August 17, 1889, North Musselshell at Martindale was flowing at the rate of 15 second-feet and South Musselshell 10 second-feet. On the same day Lebo creek was discharging 8 second-feet, American fork 3 second-feet, and Elk creek 10 second-feet. This portion of the drainage basin is in Meagher county. Farther down the stream, in Fergus county, the demand for water is even greater than at points higher on the stream, as the valley is broader, and there are thousands of acres of arable land which could be covered by canals. The tributaries which enter the Musselshell in the lower portion of its course all come from the Big Snowy mountains and contribute water only in times of flood. During the summer all of the amount available is used for irrigation on the ranches near the foothills of these mountains.

The country on both sides of the Missouri river, from above the mouth of the Judith river down to the Musselshell and even to the junction of the Yellowstone, consists largely of bad lands, in which there is no water, except in a few streams, which are from 50 to 200 feet lower than the land. There is some level land on the divide, but it is useless on account of the absence of water.

MILK RIVER.

Milk river rises in the Rocky mountains near the northern border of Montana, the greater part of the headwaters being within the Dominion of Canada, in the territory of Alberta. It flows in a general easterly direction, being in the middle third of its course nearly parallel to the Missouri, and finally turning toward the south enters the latter stream about 120 miles above the junction with the Yellowstone. For nearly its whole length it flows through prairies or high plains, from which it receives little water. The greater part of the drainage area in Montana has been until within a few years included in a vast Indian reservation, and therefore agriculture has not had an opportunity to develop. By the throwing open of the Milk River valley to settlement, however, rapid progress has been made and the possibilities of the region have begun to attract attention.

Previous to the throwing open of the Indian reservation in Milk River valley there had been experiments in farming made by white men living in the reservation, and also by the Indians, dependence for water supply being placed upon melting snow and rainfall. A crop raised in 1888 demonstrated that all kinds of grain and vegetables, flax, hemp, and to a limited extent fruit, can be produced. Water can be taken from Milk river in many places by ditches, but the stream becomes very low after the spring freshets.

The whole of the eastern end of the Missouri basin is a vast prairie country with scanty vegetation, and is in general suitable only for pasturage. There are a few localities where water can be diverted from the main stream or held in reservoirs and small patches of low land brought under irrigation. While these areas are of themselves important in this vast extent of pasture land, yet in size they are almost insignificant. There is occasionally a year during which crops can be raised without the application of water, but the uncertainty is so great that it would be ruinous for a farmer to attempt to make a living in this way. The small creeks shown on the map as draining the eastern part of the basin are usually dry for a great part of the year, although at certain times they carry a large amount of water. No measurements have been made of the amount of water available in the Milk river or in any of these streams. The Missouri river itself has been gauged at various points along this part of its course by officers of the Missouri River Commission in the course of their surveys for the purpose of improving navigation. The results of these measurements are noted on page 237 of the third annual report.[1] As there stated, the estimated mean daily discharge in 1879 was 13,530 second-feet, and in 1880 was 18,151 second-feet. As is obvious, this amount of water is far in excess of any demands which could ever be made for the purposes of irrigation.

YELLOWSTONE RIVER BASIN.

LOCATION.

The drainage basin of the Yellowstone river, as shown by the small index map, Fig. 51, lies south and partly east of the Missouri basin, above described. Continuing in order around the basin, on the east are the head waters or streams flowing into the Missouri in the Dakotas and Nebraska; on the south is the basin of the Platte and that of the Colorado, and on the southwest the tributaries of Snake river, one of the branches of the Columbia. The Yellowstone basin is separated from the head waters of the Colorado and Columbia by the continental divide, which in this portion of its course is made up in places of a high, undulating country, in which the line of water parting is not sharply defined.

The Yellowstone river rises in the national park to which the stream has given its name, flows north through deep canyons into the state of Montana, and then pursues a general northeasterly course to the junction with the Missouri river near Fort Buford, a few miles east of the state line between North Dakota and Montana. The principal tributary of the Yellowstone, the Bighorn, rises in the Wind River mountains, near the center of Wyoming, and, flowing northerly, unites with the Yellowstone about halfway from its source to mouth. Other streams, as, for example, the Tongue and Powder rivers, flow from Wyoming in a northerly course, parallel to that of the Bighorn, entering at points below the mouth of the latter stream.

As will be seen by inspection of the map, Pl. CIX, the Yellowstone river flows along the northern side of its drainage basin, its water being received almost entirely from rivers coming in from the south and heading in the Absaroka and Bighorn ranges. The east and west line forming the boundary between the states of Wyoming and Montana cuts across the headwaters of all these streams, so that as a broad statement it may be said that three-fourths of the water in the Yellowstone comes from the state of Wyoming, while the largest extent of irrigable land is probably in Montana.

---

[1] Twelfth Ann. Rept. U. S. Geol. Survey, 1890-91, pt. II, Irrigation.

AREA AND TOPOGRAPHY.

The total area of this basin is approximately 69,683 square miles, of which 36,312 square miles, or a little over one-half, are in the state of Montana. Measuring the elevation of the basin as shown by the contour lines on the map, it has been found that the areas at various altitudes are as follows:

	Square miles.
Area under 2,000 feet	200
Area from 2,000 to 3,000 feet	6,340
Area from 3,000 to 4,000 feet	12,288
Area from 4,000 to 5,000 feet	12,265
Area from 5,000 to 7,000 feet	23,605
Area over 7,000 feet	14,985

In general outline the basin, as shown by the map, is rudely triangular, a long point extending toward the northeast. All of the high ground is in the opposite direction, namely, near the **southwestern side**, the basin as a whole falling off rapidly toward the **region of the great plains of the Dakotas and eastern** Montana. The high mountains in the elevated portions of the basin, rising to altitudes of 10,000 feet and over, furnish a large and perennial supply to the streams, so that, although the drainage area is less, the amount discharged by the Yellowstone at the junction of the two streams is probably nearly equal to that flowing in the Missouri.

One of the chief characteristics of this basin is the great extent and elevation of these mountain masses occupying the southwestern part of the area. These fall into two groups, separated by the Bighorn river, **the first of these being** the Absaroka range, together with the Snowy mountains on the north **and** the Wind river range on the south, and second, the Bighorn **range, lying far to** the east. These great mountain masses receive an amount of precipitation unusually **large** for the arid region. The **greater part** of this comes in the form of snow, which, melting during the summer, **furnishes** a large amount of **water to** the widely distributed streams flowing **out in all directions**. Thus owing to the **excellent** water supply there are unusual opportunities for the development of irrigation wherever **arable land is to be found**.

In the northeastern part of the basin are plains deeply cut by the larger rivers issuing from the mountains and **also by the streams** which at **certain times of the year carry away the storm** water of the comparatively level country. On the eastern edge of the basin the plains have been deeply eroded and begin to pass into the condition of "bad **lands**," a type of country which prevails in **the vicinity** of the Black Hills.

The lofty slopes of the mountain ranges are thickly clothed with timber, some of it of great value, becoming more so as settlement advances. **The map, Pl. CIX,** has been colored to show the general distribution of this timber and also of the areas containing a notable amount of wood suitable for fuel. The remainder of the drainage **basin consists for the**

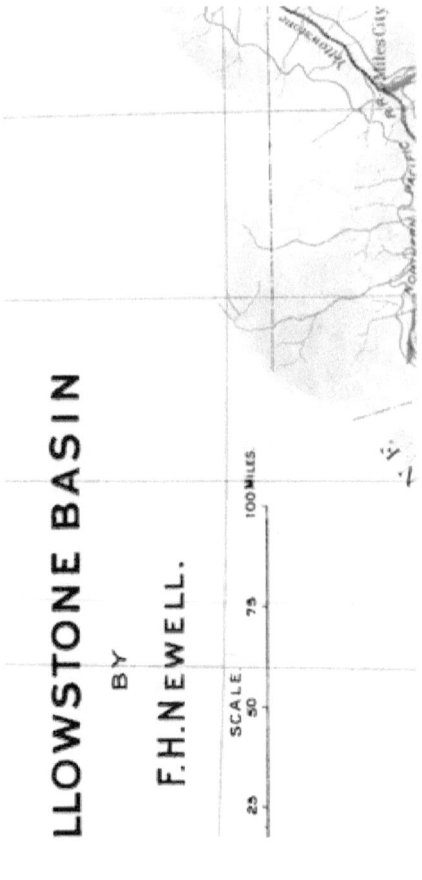

YELLOWSTONE BASIN
BY
F. H. NEWELL

SCALE
25 50 75 100 MILES

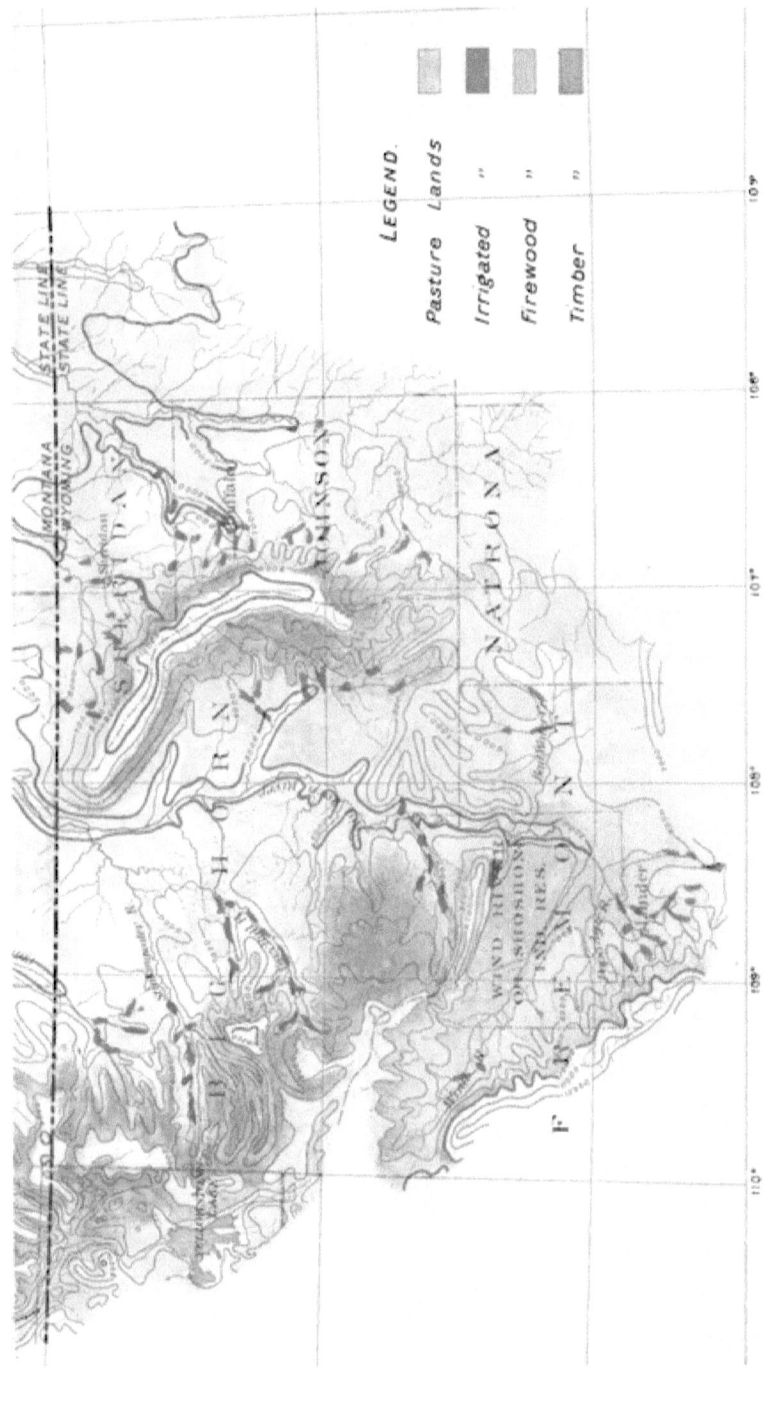

most part of grazing or hay lands, there being few localities in which food for cattle can not be found during a part of the year at least. The area covered in whole or in part by timber has been estimated to be 11,320 square miles, and by scattering firewood 13,580 square miles, leaving 44,783 square miles suitable for grazing, a small part of this being so situated that it can be brought under cultivation by irrigation.

AREA IRRIGATED.

In this basin the total area irrigated and from which crops were obtained in 1889, as shown by the Eleventh census, was 108,934 acres, or 170·21 square miles. This is only 0·38 per cent of the total area considered as pasture land, the soil of most of which is fertile and only needs the application of water to produce good crops. There are within the basin a few localities where farmers are moderately successful without irrigation, but these cases are considered as exceptional, for, as a rule, the rainfall, although heaviest in the summer season, is insufficient for the needs of most crops.

The places at which irrigation has been carried on are shown on the map by the dark spots, the area of these, however, not being in true proportion, but are somewhat exaggerated in order to make them apparent. Along the rivers a portion of the lower land has been distinguished by a different tint to indicate the irrigable areas or lands to which water may be brought in the future, the area and location of these depending of course upon the manner in which the water supply is utilized.

WATER MEASUREMENTS.

The measurements of the amount of water flowing in the Yellowstone made by the Geological Survey have been described in the previous report[1] where are also given the results of four gaugings made below Yellowstone lake. In addition measurements have been made by officers of the Engineer Corps, U. S. Army, giving the total amount of water carried at various points on the main stream.[2] One of these, made at the junction of the Bighorn and Yellowstone in August, 1879, showed that the Yellowstone above the Bighorn was discharging at the rate of 7,471 second-feet and the Bighorn 5,865 second-feet, making the total discharge below this point 13,336 second-feet. Further down stream, at Fort Keogh, above Miles City, in September, 1878, the discharge was 14,462 second-feet, and in October, 1879, 6,505 second-feet, showing a comparatively wide range for the late summer season. At Wolf rapids, about a mile below the mouth of Powder river, the discharge in September, 1878, was 11,235 second-feet, and at Diamond island, about 30 miles above the junction of the Missouri, the discharge

---

[1] Eleventh Ann. Rept. U. S. Geol. Survey, pt. II, Irrigation, pp. 36-38; see also tables in Appendix of this report, p. 93.

[2] Ann. Rept. Chief of Eng., U. S. Army, 1880, p. 1476. See also report for 1879, p. 1101, and for 1883, p. 1351. For distances, fall, and rate of fall per mile see report for 1880, p. 1477.

in October, 1878, was 8,155 second-feet. The above, with one gauging of the Bighorn made by W. H. Graves, engineer of the Indian bureau, comprise nearly all the data available. This latter measurement of the Bighorn was made near the mouth of the canyon on September 4, 1891. The width of the river was 257 feet, the average depth 2·91 feet, the rate of flow 4·28 feet per second, and the computed discharge 3,200 second-feet. The drainage basin at this locality is about 18,000 square miles, and the average fall from the canyon down to Fort Custer 7 feet per mile.

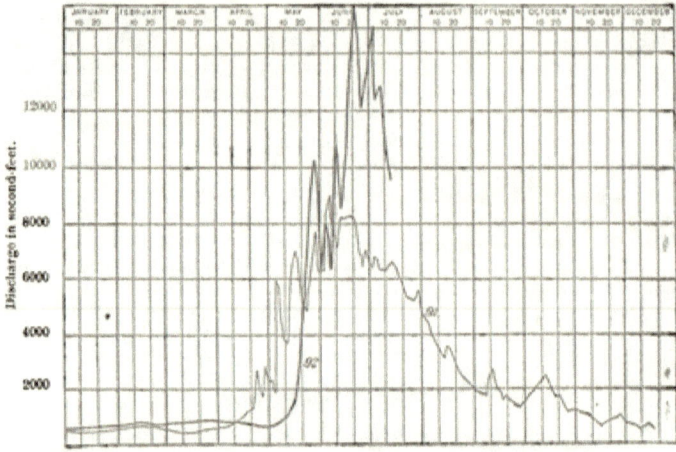

FIG. 56.—Diagram of daily discharge of Yellowstone river near Horr, Montana, for 1891 and 1892.

Observations of the height of the river at Horr, about 4 miles below Cinnabar, have been made by the Geological Survey since August, 1889, giving data from which to compute the daily discharge as shown on Fig. 56.[1] Above this point the water has not been diverted, a great part of the area drained being within the Yellowstone National park. The features of this wonderful country have been described in many publications, notably in the volumes of the U. S. Geological and Geographical Survey of the Territories, commonly known as the "Hayden Survey," from its chief, Dr. F. V. Hayden. In this connection it is sufficient to state that the catchment basin of the river above Horr consists of a high volcanic plateau, situated at a mean elevation of about 8,000 feet, surrounded by rugged mountain ranges whose summits rise to altitudes of from 10,000 to 11,000 feet and over above sea level. Yellowstone lake is a natural reservoir tending to equalize the flow of the river and in which if necessary an enormous amount of water could be held at relatively small expense. It is doubtful, however, whether this will ever be desirable, since the Yellowstone River carries an amount

---

[1] See also Twelfth Ann. Rept. U. S. Geol. Survey, Pl. LXIV, p. 236.

of water far in excess of **the needs of the lands which can be brought
under ditch by ordinary means.**

A few measurements were made at Springdale, east of Livingston,
and about 70 miles below Horr, but the results at this place did not
materially differ from those at Horr, and therefore work at that point
was abandoned. **Near the** headwaters of the Tongue **and Powder**
rivers the state engineer of Wyoming has made a number of gaugings
of streams of importance in irrigation. A brief statement of the results
of these measurements is given further on in the description of the
basins of the rivers mentioned.

As a general statement it may be said that the amount of water in
the Yellowstone and its principal tributary, the Bighorn, is far **in excess of any demand to be made upon it.** It does not seem credible **that**
irrigation works will ever be constructed of **a** magnitude such that a
serious diminution of the annual discharge will take **place.** In the case
of the small tributaries, however, **issuing from the eastern** side of the
Absaroka and other ranges of this group and from the **Bighorn** mountains, where the supply, though in the aggregate large, is well distrib**uted,** the amount ordinarily available is not sufficient for all demands.
In these localities are many valleys where on account of the rapid fall
of the streams water can be readily diverted upon arable lands and in the
aggregate thousands of acres brought under cultivation. It is in such
places that economy in the use of water must be observed and the **summer flow increased,** if possible, by the construction of storage **reservoirs.**

PRECIPITATION.

In the Yellowstone basin there are comparatively few localities at
which measurements of the amount of rainfall have been made. The
longest records are those which have been kept by post surgeons at
various camps and forts. From these records, collected and published
by the Signal Service of the Army, it is apparent that the annual precipitation ranges from 10 inches on the plains in the northeastern part
of the basin up to 30 inches or over in the valleys among the mountains.
No observations have been made as to the depth of precipitation on the
high summits, but it is probable that it amounts to as much as 40
inches or **even more.**

In the following list are given **the names of the principal** stations at
which measurements have been made, together with the number of
years and **the average** depth of precipitation:

Locality.	Length of record.	Average depth of rainfall.
	Years.	Inches.
Camp Sheridan, near Mammoth Hot springs, Yellowstone National park	2	25.46
Fort Washakie, 15 miles northwest of Lander, Wyoming	9	10.14
Fort McKinney, at Buffalo, Wyoming	4	10.53
Fort Custer, Montana, at mouth of Little Bighorn	10	13.16
Fort Keogh, near Miles, Montana	12	12.96
Glendive, Montana	2	10.15

The first of these stations, that in the Yellowstone National park, is at an altitude of over 6,300 feet, and is surrounded by high peaks, and thus, as might be expected, the amount of precipitation is relatively great. Most of this comes in the winter months, and in this respect differs from records at other localities in the basin. The distribution of rainfall during the year at these places is similar in most respects to that in the Missouri basin, the greater part of the rainfall occurring in May and June, as shown graphically on Fig. 52.

Taking the mean monthly rainfall at the stations named above, excepting Camp Sheridan, the precipitation per month obtained by averaging these is as follows:

	Inches.	Per cent.
January	0·64	5·7
February	0·50	4·5
March	0·56	5·0
April	1·05	9·4
May	2·13	19·1
June	1·88	16·9
July	1·25	11·2
August	0·92	8·3
September	0·86	7·7
October	0·67	6·0
November	0·36	3·2
December	0·34	3·0
Total	11·16	100·0

YELLOWSTONE RIVER ABOVE BIGHORN.

In a detailed description of the water supply of the Yellowstone basin it becomes convenient to divide the whole area into a number of sub-basins, each embracing the catchment of a large tributary or a portion of the main stream. The first of these sub-basins may be taken as that portion of the Yellowstone basin which includes the headwaters down to the mouth of the Bighorn river. Next in geographic order on the east is the basin of the Bighorn, succeeded by those of the Tongue and of the Powder river, and finally the remaining area tributary to the lower part of the main stream.

The general character of the catchment basin of the Upper Yellowstone has been briefly described above. After leaving the great canyons below the National park the river flows through a narrow valley, in which a small amount of irrigation is practiced, mainly by means of water from mountain streams. At the northern end of this valley the river passes through the lower canyon and shortly beyond this locality takes a general course toward the east, the lowlands becoming wider and better adapted for agricultural purposes. As shown by the map, the river partially encircles the northern end of the Absaroka or Snowy range, receiving from these lofty mountains a great number of streams which flow out toward almost every point of the compass, emptying directly into the Yellowstone, or, uniting, form large tributaries, such, for example, as Clarke Fork. These streams carry a perennial supply of water, which is utilized wherever possible upon the lowlands in the narrow valleys. The streams coming into the river from **the lower** mountain ranges on **the left** hand, viz, the western or **northern side,** discharge a relatively small amount of water, the quantity **being far** less than that needed to supply the agricultural land, and as **a consequence** there have been quarrels and expensive litigation concerning **the division of** water. In a number of instances attempts have **been** made to increase the summer discharge of small streams by the **construction** of storage reservoirs **by** farmers, **working** singly or in **partnership.**

Little if any **water is** taken from the main river until a point about 30 miles above Billings is reached. At and below this point are a number of canals and ditches on the north **side** covering land in the vicinity of Park city, and from thence down to Billings. The principal of these in order are the canal of the Minnesota and Montana Land and Improvement Company, the Italian Company's ditch, **Mill ditch,** Clarkes Fork ditch, and the Yellowstone and Canyon creek ditch.

Clarkes fork enters the Yellowstone from the **south side about 10** miles east of Park city. It discharges a large quantity of water, the amount of which has not been ascertained. Irrigation is carried on at various places along the head waters in Bighorn county, Wyoming, but owing to the fact that the stream throughout its course in Montana **is** within the **area lately** a part of the Crow Indian reservation the waters in that State have **not been** utilized.

BIGHORN RIVER.

The Bighorn river rises on the northeasterly side of the Wind river **mountains and** flows northerly between the Bighorn and Absaroka **ranges,** receiving many large tributaries from **both of** these great mountain masses. The water supply is in excess **of any** demands likely **to be** made upon it for many years, owing **to the fact** that the larger bodies of agricultural land along its course **can** only be reached by long and expensive canals. The greater part of **this** basin is comparatively inaccessible, owing to the distance from **lines of transportation.** The principal industries are mining **and stock** raising, a small amount of irrigation being practiced on lands mainly near mining camps or on the low grounds of cattle ranches. The White river or Shoshone Indian reservation in Wyoming and the Crow Indian reservation in **Montana** cover some of the best land in this basin, but outside of **these are many** localities to which water can profitably be brought.

The greater part of the irrigation is in the vicinity of Lander, **south** of the Wind river reservation, water for the cultivated lands being taken from the Popo Agie and its tributaries. From this point northerly along the base of the mountains **on** both sides of the river water has been diverted in a small way from the head waters of the Wind river, Owl **creek, Grey** Bull, Badwater, and other streams. **There are** no large canals, but many ditches dug by individuals or by **a number of irrigators acting in partnership.**

Measurements of the amount **of water in** many of the small streams in the vicinity of **Lander were made by the** state engineer during the summer of 1892,[1] **the principal results** of which are given in round numbers in the following table:

Date.	Stream.	Discharge in second-feet.
June 19, 1892	Beaver creek, at Hailey	70
June 23, 1892	Squaw creek	26
June 27, 1892	Mexican creek	6
July 5, 1892	North Fork Popo Agie river, at Milford bridge	619
July 20, 1892	Middle Fork Popo Agie river, near Lander	343
Aug. 4, 1892	Little Popo Agie river	67
Aug. 8, 1892	Cherry creek	9
Aug. 8, 1892	Red Canyon creek	5

A few measurements were also made about this time giving the discharge of Bighorn river at the ferry at Alamo in Bighorn county. The results showed that on July 10 the mean velocity at this point was 4.72 feet per second, and the total discharge 9,707 second-feet. On July 14 the Stinking Water river at the bride at Corbett had a mean velocity of 6.22 feet per second and was discharging 4,974 second-feet, this water entering the Bighorn about 45 miles below Alamo.

Within the Crow Indian reservation in Montana a small amount of irrigation has been carried on by Indians by use of water from the Little Bighorn. This stream receives water from the northern end of the Bighorn range, and is of sufficient size to irrigate a large acreage. Surveys have been made under the direction of the Indian Bureau, and estimates prepared of the expense of canals in order to determine the feasibility of systems of irrigation supplied with water from the Bighorn and from the Little Bighorn. It has been ascertained that water can be diverted upon the highlands between the two streams or upon those to the west of the main river at a cost per acre sufficiently low to justify construction.

TONGUE RIVER.

The Tongue river heads on the northeasterly slopes of the Bighorn range in Sheridan county, Wyoming. Below the junction of its principal tributaries the river flows in a direction a little east of north through Custer county, Montana, entering the Yellowstone. Irrigation is carried on in Wyoming to a large and constantly increasing extent by means of the many streams draining the high mountains, these being widely distributed and easily diverted upon land among the foothills. On account of this fact Sheridan county is rapidly becoming one of the principal agricultural localities of the state. In the aggregate, however, there is more good farming land than can

---

[1] First biennial report of the state engineer to the governor of Wyoming, 1891 and 1892. Cheyenne, Wyoming, 1892. **Appendix, p. xxi.**

be irrigated, and along some of the small streams there is occasionally a scanty supply. Gaugings of a few of the more important streams have been made by Prof. Elwood Mead, state engineer of Wyoming. The data[1] furnished by him show that on June 29, 1891, Little Goose creek at Davis ranch discharged 109 second-feet; on July 5, 1889, Big Goose creek at Beckton bridge discharged 169 second-feet and on July 1, 1893, at Sheridan bridge, 1,009 second-feet; on July 29, 1891, Tongue river at Dayton bridge discharged 192 second-feet, and on July 28 the south fork of Tongue river at Burkitt's flume discharged 18 second-feet.

Outside of the foothills it becomes a matter of considerable trouble and expense to divert the water, on account of the banks of the stream in most cases being high and the material of such a nature that it washes away or softens under the action of water. The river is very crooked, crossing the bottom lands from bluff to bluff, rendering it expensive and even impossible to build long ditches. With increase of population, however, it will doubtless be practicable to attempt large schemes to cover the higher lands and utilize most of the water in the main stream.

In its course through Montana there is comparatively little irrigation along the river. A few ditches have been dug, but there are not many localities where water can be diverted at small expense. Attempts have been made to use pumps in order to lift the water up to the top of the steep banks. The bottom lands are usually narrow and so frequently cut by the river in its course from side to side that ditches can not be built. At Miles is the largest ditch along the lower course of the Tongue river. This heads on the east side of the river about 15 miles above the Yellowstone and follows down along the stream to Miles, where it turns off into the valley of the Yellowstone. The water in Tongue river is raised by a dam to a height of about 7 feet above low water, diverting it into the canal.

Between the Bighorn and Powder rivers is the Rosebud, which flows northerly into the Yellowstone. This river does not head in the high mountains, and therefore during a large part of the year is nearly dry. There are probably twenty ditches along the stream, irrigating small areas of hay, grain, and vegetables. In July, August, and September the water often ceases to run, and for sometime during late spring the creek furnishes barely enough for the land under cultivation, so that it will be necessary to store some of the water which flows to waste in the early part of the year in order to utilize a considerable proportion of the agricultural land in this valley.

POWDER RIVER.

The Powder river receives the greater part of its water from the eastern side of the Bighorn range, its upper tributaries being south of those of Tongue river. These are utilized for irrigation at points along

---

[1] First biennial report of the state engineer to the governor of Wyoming, 1891 and 1892. Cheyenne, Wyo., 1892. Appendix, pp. XIX and XXI.

the foothills where they can be readily diverted, a **comparatively small amount of** water escaping to the main river during the irrigating season. The ditches highest **up on the** stream receive usually an abundant supply, while those lower down are often short of water, causing **many controversies** which require the intervention of state officers. In **1889 there was an** unusual drought, and many of the upper streams, especially those receiving water from **the lower foothills, were entirely dry, resulting in large losses of crops. At a distance of from 20 to 50 miles from the mountains the waters of the various streams are fully appropriated,** and in many cases the amount called for is far in **excess of** the ordinary discharge. The measurements made by Prof. **Elwood Mead**[1] show that **on** June 3, 1891, Clear creek, at weir in the canyon, discharged 552 second-feet, and on **August 3, at the** same place, **72 second-feet;** also, **on** August 12, Rock **creek below** the forks, near Buffalo, Johnson county, **discharged 17** second-feet. Many other streams were measured, the result in each case being less than 5 second-feet.

As the Powder river and its tributaries leave the vicinity of the mountains the amount **of** water available decreases, the expense of taking it out upon the land becomes greater, and long before reaching the Montana line **no irrigation is** attempted. In its course through Custer county **in the latter state the river during a great part of the year ceases to flow,** and owing to the character of the country irrigation **is practically impossible. This part of the basin of the Yellowstone is within the "bad lands," and has little or no value for agriculture or stock-raising.**

LOWER YELLOWSTONE RIVER.

From Billings down to the mouth of the river there are at intervals small areas of irrigated land, **these being mainly at places where tributaries** enter from the north or south. **The amount of water in the river,** as shown by the measurements previously **mentioned, is very great, but** none of this has been diverted by canals **on account of the very gentle** fall of the stream. In a few localities pumps have **been erected and sufficient** water raised to cover small gardens or to irrigate **trees.** The **side streams,** however, have a greater slope and can be controlled by **dams raising** the water above the level of the lower land. The largest **system of irrigation is that** previously mentioned as being in the vicinity **of Miles.**

On account of the great expense of building canals to cover the low land along the Yellowstone many of the farmers have been compelled to resort to what are known as **"high-water" ditches.** These are dug at places where during the high water of spring they will receive some

---

[1] First biennial report of the state engineer **to the governor** of Wyoming, 1891 and 1892. Cheyenne, Wyo., 1892. Appendix, p. xix.

of the overflow, carrying it out upon grounds farther down the stream. In this way a large acreage, mainly of hay land, can be given one thorough soaking. Beyond the bottom lands are vast areas of fertile land lying at a height above the river so great that it is improbable that water can ever be brought to them. To irrigate these plains would necessitate the construction of a canal of 100 miles at least in length, and if practicable the expense will doubtless be too great for any ordinary corporation to undertake. To determine the feasibility of such a canal will require careful surveys and a thorough examination of the matter from all standpoints.

PLATTE RIVER BASIN.

LOCATION AND AREA.

The drainage basin of the Platte above the junction of the north and south branches lies mainly in southeastern Wyoming and northern Colorado, a small portion being within the state of Nebraska. As shown by the index map, Fig. 51, this basin on the northwest adjoins that of the Yellowstone. On the west are the headwaters of the Colorado river, on the south those of the Arkansas, and on the northeast and southeast are the streams which, coming from springs on the Great Plains, flow easterly into the Missouri river. The basin as a whole, as shown by Pl. CX, slopes from the mountains in the southwestern part, both north and easterly, the greatest fall being in the latter direction.

The total area of this basin is 57,320 square miles, of which 24,240 square miles are in Wyoming, 22,230 square miles in Colorado, and 10,850 square miles in Nebraska. Of the area in Colorado 2,025 square miles are included within the drainage basin of the North Platte and 20,205 square miles in that of the South Platte, this latter basin being thus almost entirely within Colorado. The line of watershed of the basins of the North and South Platte is not sharply defined, except among the high mountains. Throughout the Great Plains it is very indefinite, and also in the high almost desert area in Sweetwater county, Wyoming. A somewhat arbitrary line has, therefore, been taken as bounding these sides.

The North Platte rises in the northern part of the main range of the Rocky mountains in Colorado and flows in a general northerly course nearly half across Wyoming. The direction taken by this part of the river shows plainly the general slope of the surface of Wyoming toward the north. A relatively slight depression of the central part of the state would throw the waters of this stream directly into the headwaters of Powder river, which flows northerly on the prolongation of the course taken by the upper part of the North Platte. This latter river, however, shortly after receiving the Sweetwater from the west, begins to swing around toward the east, flowing along the upper edge of the drainage basin, and, having described nearly a half circle around the Laramie hills, takes a **southeasterly course** and flows for over 150 miles in an almost **straight line**. The **principal** tributary, the Laramie river, curves in a manner similar to that of the upper waters of the **North Platte**. It rises behind the **Laramie range**, flows northerly, and then **gradually turns toward the east, passing through** the range to join the main river.

The **South Platte** rises behind the **Front range of the Rocky mountains** and, passing out through a **canyon, flows along the foothills,** collecting in its northerly course the **waters of a large number of mountain creeks**, each of which issues through a deep **canyon**. After receiving the **Cache la** Poudre, the largest stream of this part of the country, the **river turns toward** the east and flows out through the **Great Plains**. As the **North** and the South Platte continue on their way through the comparatively level country they converge at first rapidly and then more and **more** slowly, flowing within a few miles of each **other for a** distance of over 50 miles, **the bed of** the South Platte being probably slightly higher **than** that of the **North** Platte.

ELEVATION AND TOPOGRAPHY.

The general elevation of the basin is best shown by the following table, prepared by means of measurements of the areas inclosed by contour lines on Pl. CX, this plate being a portion of the large map of the United States compiled by Henry Gannett. The line of the divide, as previously stated, has been arbitrarily assumed in various parts of the more level country.

	Square miles.
Total area	57,320
Area under 3,000 feet	700
Area from 3,000 to 4,000 feet	5,960
Area from 4,000 to 5,000 feet	14,660
Area from 5,000 to 7,000 feet	21,660
Area above 7,000 feet	14,340

The basin as a whole is among the most elevated in the country, an almost insignificant portion, that near the junction of the two branches, being under 3,000 feet. From this point the country gradually rises, preserving the character of a plain until the altitude of 7,000 feet or **over is reached,** the base of the mountains being at about this elevation **above sea level. On** the northern side of the basin the undulating or **slightly broken** plains, **mainly under** 7,000 feet in altitude, sweep **around through** the ranges of the Rocky mountains to the head waters **of streams flowing into** the Pacific or into the Great Interior basin, **and a traveler can pass over the** continental divide almost without seeing a mountain peak except **in the** far distance. In the south half of the basin, however, the Front range of the Rockies presents a bold face to the east and apparently blocks advance toward the west. These

U.S. GEOLOGICAL SURVEY.

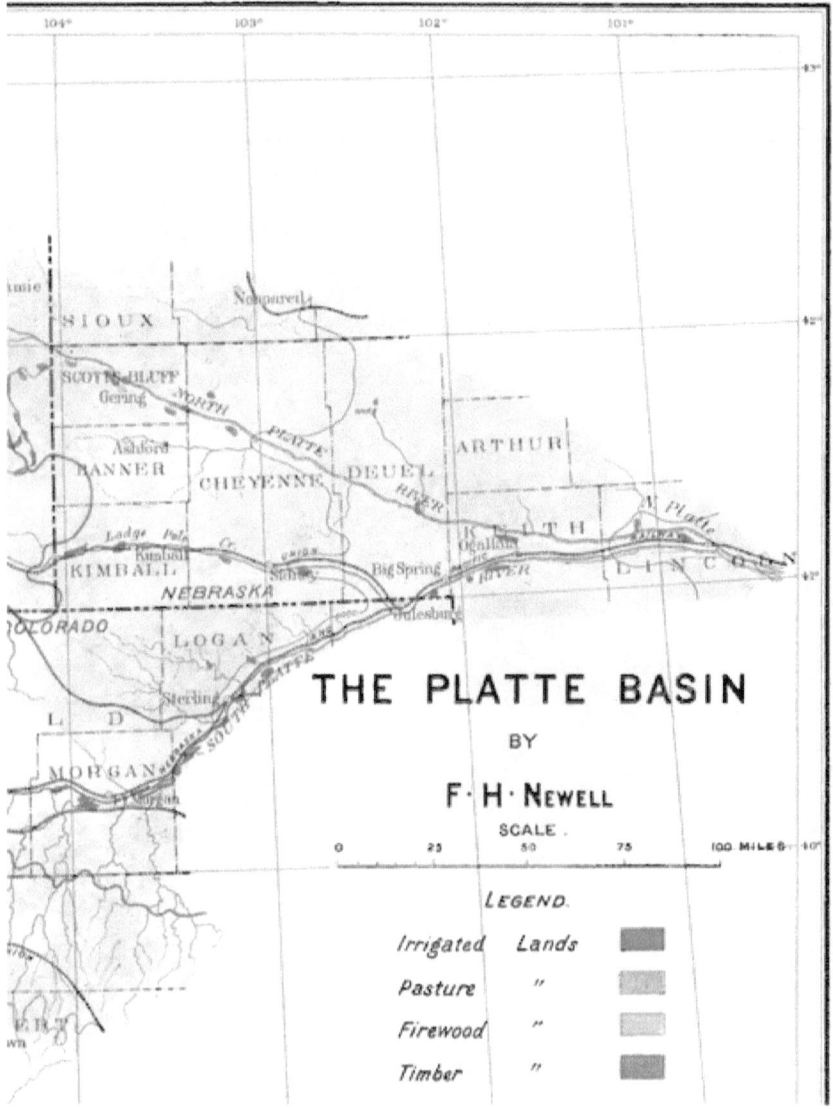

mountains and those to the rear rise to altitudes of from 10,000 to 12,000 feet or more, and their peaks are for a great part of the year covered with snow. Among these are broad parks whose bottom lands are 8,000 feet or more in height. From the North park comes the North Platte, from the Middle park the Grand river, flowing into the Colorado, and from the South park the head waters of the South Platte. These and other smaller valleys are traversed by many streams, and besides furnishing excellent grazing produce large quantities of hay.

LAND CLASSIFICATION.

Plate CX has been colored to represent in a general way the character of the country. The darker color represents the area upon which forests suitable for timber have grown, while the lighter shade covers the areas within which trees fit only for firewood are to be found. The uncolored portion on the western end of the map is the high desert region, upon which there is very little, if any, forage. The rest of the basin may be considered as suitable for grazing, and in most places the soil, if watered, is excellent for farming purposes.

The total area of the timber land as shown by the map is 5,380 square miles; of the firewood, 4,820 square miles, and of the desert area, about 3,000 square miles, leaving in the basin a total of 44,120 square miles of grazing and agricultural land, this latter area being distinguished by the brownish tint. Within this are spots indicated by a dark color showing the relative location of lands under cultivation by irrigation, and along the streams mainly are strips of lighter tint, showing lands which possibly may be brought under irrigation by a thorough utilization of the water supply.

EXTENT OF IRRIGATION.

The total area upon which crops were raised by irrigation in 1889 was, as shown by the Eleventh Census, 542,602 acres. Of this amount 412,683 acres were in Colorado, 120,893 acres in Wyoming, and 9,026 acres in Nebraska. As shown by the map, Pl. CX, these areas are clustered around the base of the mountain ranges where the streams issue from the canyon or broken ground out upon the edge of the plains. There are also a few localities further down stream where water has been diverted, but these are relatively of less importance, largely on account of the fact that little dependence can be placed upon the supply of water during summer.

As a rule it may be said that wherever water can be obtained and brought out at moderate expense upon arable land this has already been done. On all of the minor streams of the basin an amount of water is claimed to exceed that which ordinarily can be found in them. Cultivation has advanced to such an extent that during the summer there is not sufficient water available to fill the demands of the farmers. The principal exception is in the case of the North Platte, where there is always a surplus of water, but which, however, can only be utilized by the construction of extensive systems of irrigation.

The basin of the Platte, especially that of the south branch of the river, contains some of the largest irrigating canals in the United States, and the development of agriculture by the artificial application of water has been brought to a state as high, if not higher, than that of any other part of the country, excepting possibly California. In Wyoming there still remain opportunities for the development of large systems of irrigation, but in Colorado canals have been built at nearly every favorable locality and the aggregate capacity of these is so great that it is improbable that they can receive water sufficient to supply all of the agricultural land which can be reached by them.

WATER MEASUREMENTS.

Measurements of the amount of water flowing at various points on the creeks and rivers of this basin have been made by the state engineers of Colorado and Wyoming, and the water supply is probably better known than that of any other area of its size. In Colorado some of these measurements and continuous computations of discharge date from 1884, and in Wyoming from 1887, thus giving in one or two instances the spring and summer discharge through eight years. The results of the work of the state engineers of Colorado are to be found in the biennial reports to the governor of the state, and those for Wyoming in part in the first and second annual report of the territorial engineer and also in the first biennial report of the state engineer. In addition to these data results of a number of gaugings are to be found in reports by Henry Gannett in the Hayden reports for 1876 and 1877,[1] and also in the annual reports of the present Geological Survey. All of these will be discussed in the following pages under the head of the various subbasins in which they were obtained.

PRECIPITATION.

In this basin and in most of those of the western half of the United States there are few records giving the monthly and annual rainfall for any considerable number of years. The Signal Service of the Army has, however, brought together and published all of the data available, and from these tables the following condensed statement has been obtained.[2] The mean annual rainfall is given only for the places hav-

---

[1] U. S. Geol. and Geog. Survey of Colorado and adjacent territory, 1876. F. V. Hayden. Washington, 1878, pp. 311-347. Also U. S. Geol. and Geog. Survey of the territories of Idaho and Wyoming, 1877. F. V. Hayden, Washington, 1879, pp. 673-710.

[2] Irrigation and water storage in the arid regions, by Gen. A. W. Greely, chief signal officer, Ex. Doc. No. 287, House, Fifty-first Congress, second session, Washington, 1891. Climate of Nebraska, Ex. Doc. No. 115, Senate, Fifty-first Congress, first session, 1890. Rainfall on the Pacific slope, etc., Ex. Doc. No. 91, Senate, Fiftieth Congress, first session, 1888.

ing the longest record, stations where observations have been carried on for one or two years only being omitted. The order given is, in general, that from west to east.

Locality.	Length of record.	Average depth of rainfall.
	Years.	Inches.
Fort Fred Steele, Wyo., 25 miles below Saratoga	12	11.02
Fort Sanders, 3 miles south of Laramie City, Wyo	9	12.93
Fort Fetterman, 8 miles above Douglas, Wyo	12	15.06
Fort Laramie, Wyo	26	12.30
Cheyenne, Wyo	20	11.68
Fort Collins, Colo	19	13.75
Golden, Colo	12	17.55
Denver, Colo	22	14.32
Colorado Springs, Colo	20	14.79
Pikes Peak, Colo	15	28.65
Fort Morgan, Colo	7	8.08
Fort Sedgwick and Julesburg, Colo	7	15.80
Sidney, Nebr	12	14.23
North Platte, Nebr	16	19.18
Fort McPherson, Nebr	13	17.96
Redwillow, Nebr	5	21.77
Fort Kearney, Nebr	17	25.44

The highest of these stations, that on Pikes peak, is at an altitude of 14,134 feet, and the lowest, Fort Kearney, Nebraska, is 2,360 feet. The other stations range from 3,000 up to 7,000 feet, as shown by the contoured map. It is evident from an inspection of the table that the mean annual precipitation over the greater part of the basin is less than 15 inches, the amount varying from about 30 inches on the summits of the mountains down to from 12 to 15 inches at their base. On going away from the mountains down the slope of the plains the mean annual rainfall decreases for some distance, and as progress is made toward the subhumid regions the quantity increases up to 20 inches or more. In other words, as is well known, the least rainfall is to be found along the western border of the Great plains at a short distance from the base of the mountains.

The distribution of rainfall by months is quite uniform over the basin, being similar in character to that prevailing in the adjoining drainage basins. By taking data given for the stations above mentioned, excepting Pikes peak, the following table has been prepared, showing the mean monthly rainfall of the localities named and the percentage that this bears to the total for the year:

	Inches.	Per cent.		Inches.	Per cent.
January	0.54	3.5	August	1.65	10.7
February	.56	3.6	September	1.16	7.6
March	.82	5.4	October	.93	6.1
April	1.76	11.5	November	.57	3.8
May	2.65	17.3	December	.58	3.8
June	1.90	12.4			
July	2.19	14.3	Total	15.31	100.0

UPPER NORTH PLATTE.

The North Platte river rises in the mountains partially surrounding the North park in the western end of Larimer county, Colorado, and, flowing northerly out of the park, traverses Carbon county, Wyoming, its course being a little west of north. Shortly after leaving Carbon county the river receives from the west the **Sweetwater**, which drains a part of the southern end of the Wind River range. Irrigation is being carried on by the utilization of nearly all of the tributaries above the Sweetwater, the water supply being comparatively large and easily available for this purpose.

The North park is at an altitude of from 7,500 feet to nearly 8,000 feet, while the mountains surrounding it rise to heights of from 12,000 to 13,000 feet above sea level. From these come almost innumerable streams tributary to one or another of the three forks which, after traversing the park converge at the lower or northern end, forming the North Platte. The surface of the park is undulating, but from an elevation appears to be quite level. The greater part is covered by native grasses, furnishing excellent grazing. The climate, however, is too cold for the general practice of agriculture. Small ditches have been dug, taking water out of the mountain streams for the purpose of irrigating forage, and according to the report of the state engineer of Colorado, over 150 of these have been recorded. The water supply is large, ample for all present needs.

At the north end of the park the Medicine Bow range on the east and the Park range on the west approach each other, the North Platte escaping through a narrow canyon between these, finally entering the broad valley. Here it receives tributaries from both mountain ranges, each stream being of value for irrigation. The general height of the farming land is a little under 7,000 feet, the altitude at Fort Steele being 6,516 feet and at Rawlins 6,754. The principal crop is hay, the cereals having a relatively small acreage.

Measurements of the amount of water available have been made by the state engineer of Wyoming, from whom have been obtained the results of various gaugings,[1] the principal of which are herewith given in geographic order. The most southerly or highest tributary measured is Brush creek, coming from the Medicine Bow range and entering the North Platte about 6 miles below the mouth of the canyon. The discharge on August 6, 1891, at Condict ranch was 34 second-feet. Below this on the opposite side are Grand Encampment and Cow creeks, the first of which on August 1 discharged 151 second-feet and the latter 14 second-feet. The next in order is South Spring creek. This on July 24, 1891, discharged at a point about 6 miles south of Saratoga 25 second-feet, and North Spring creek 15 second-feet. Jack creek westerly from Saratoga on July 17 discharged 14 second-feet,

---

[1] First biennial report of the state engineer to the governor of Wyoming, 1891 and 1892. Cheyenne, Wyo., 1892. Appendix. p. xviii.

and Pass creek 20 miles north of Saratoga on June 30 discharged 46 second-feet. The water in all of these streams diminishes rapidly in July, and during August there is often scarcity.

There are no measurements available of the amount of water in the North Platte in this part of its course, but it is known there is a large volume, and if canals can be built heading in or near the canyon and running out on each side of the valley, large tracts can be brought under irrigation. As it is at present only the lowlands along the creeks are utilized, owing to the expense involved in the construction of any comprehensive system.

The Sweetwater river, after leaving the Wind river mountains, flows in a general easterly course from Fremont county along the southern edge of Natrona county to its junction with the North Platte. This river discharges a large perennial supply of water, the amount of which is not known. Little if any irrigation is carried on along this stream, on account of the difficulty and expense of diverting the water upon the agricultural lands. The side streams, however, like those of the North Platte, are utilized wherever this can be easily done. On the broad undulating plain through which this river runs there are vast areas of fertile land lying at an altitude of a little over 6,000 feet. The soil is fertile, and were it not for the extreme aridity of the country, would be capable of producing the hardier cereals and crops of grass. It is possible that in the future canals may be built to cover some of these areas, but extensive surveys will be required before the facts can be definitely stated.

LARAMIE RIVER.

The Laramie river rises in the Medicine Bow mountains east of North park, and, flowing northerly across the State line into Wyoming, reaches the edge of the Laramie plains. From this point it turns northeasterly, crosses the plains and, as a rapid, clear stream, flows northerly near the foot of the Laramie hills through broad, grass-covered bottoms. A gauging station has been established at Woods, giving the discharge of the river as it enters upon the plains. The record kept by the State engineer of Wyoming shows that in 1889, from January to March, inclusive, the discharge was practically uniform, being about 112 second-feet. The maximum discharge, in June, was 1,620 second-feet, and the minimum, 43 second-feet, in September. A gauging on November 6, 1891, gave a discharge of 75 second-feet and on June 7, 1892, 1,571 second-feet, the mean velocity being 6·6 feet per second.

The river in its course along the Laramie plains does not receive any tributaries from the Laramie hills, and, excepting from the Little Laramie, no water enters from the creeks on the west. These latter streams, draining the Medicine Bow range, flow out upon the plains into lakes or marshes, where the water evaporates, leaving the smaller lakes at least strongly alkaline. These mountains rise to altitudes of from 3,000 to 4,000 feet above the plains, thus giving rise to large creeks, while the Laramie hills on the eastern side of the plains are relatively but low ridges, rising about 1,500 feet above the bottom lands, and the water from them flows toward the east. The Laramie plains are about 30 miles in width, and 80 miles in length from north to south, and have an average elevation of about 7,000 feet, the town of Laramie being at an altitude of 7,159 feet, according to the railroad levels. In many respects these plains, though larger, resemble the parks within the Rocky mountains. The plain with its ridges and surrounding bench lands is well covered with grass, affording excellent grazing, but owing to the climate there is little agriculture carried on, the chief industry being stock raising.

The Little Laramie river rises at about the center of Medicine Bow range, flowing easterly out upon the Laramie plains at a point west of the town of Laramie. This, as above stated, is the only stream which crosses the plains and flows into the Big Laramie. On May 28, 1891, as gauged by the state engineer, the Little Laramie at May's ranch was discharging at the rate of 562 second-feet and on June 7, 1892, at the same place, 618 second-feet. North of this is Seven Mile creek, which empties into James lake. On June 6, 1891, this was flowing at the rate of 40 second-feet, but by August 28 it was nearly or quite dry. About 3 miles further north is Four Mile creek, which on June 9, 1891, was discharging 25 second-feet. Continuing along the base of the mountains for about 8 miles Dutton creek is reached, this stream losing its water in Cooper lake. On June 12, 1891, the discharge was nearly 22 second-feet, but by the latter part of August this as well as the two creeks above named had become dry.[1] A number of ditches have been taken out of these streams, most of these being from 1 to 6 miles in length. The largest canals are those taken from Laramie river, heading at or below the canyon and continuing along the river toward the town of Laramie, one of these being over 25 miles in length. The waters of all the small streams are being utilized during the summer, and it is probable that some of the floods of spring will be saved in order to increase the acreage which can be watered during the dry season. A gauging of the amount of water in Laramie river at the town of that name was made on October 5, 1892, at which time there was found only 26 second-feet. This represents mainly the excess or seepage water from the canals covering land in the vicinity. Twenty days later the flow had increased to about 63 second-feet as shown by a measurement made by the state engineer.

After passing through or around the Laramie hills the river flows easterly out upon the Great Plains, receiving about 18 miles above its mouth Chugwater creek, which flows in from the south through a broad, fertile valley. This latter creek flows northerly along the eastern front of Laramie hills, being formed by the union of small creeks which drain

---

[1] First biennial report of the state engineer to the governor of Wyoming, 1891 and 1892. Cheyenne, Wyo., 1892. Appendix, pp. XVIII, xx.

this elevated land. Irrigation is carried on along the stream, the water supply being completely utilized, at least during the dry season. In the fertile valley of the Laramie are some of the finest irrigated lands of the state, producing large crops each year.

LOWER NORTH PLATTE.

Under this heading may be included that part of the river from the mouth of the Sweetwater down to the junction of the South Platte, comparatively little water being used from the main stream, as it is difficult to divert it. There is, however, a practically unlimited amount of arable land along the river, which, except for grazing, is worthless without irrigation. The side streams, which come in mainly from the south, are completely utilized, and more land would be brought under cultivation along the course of each if water could be had. Below the Laramie river the principal tributaries are Rawhide creek and Horse creek, both of which discharge small quantities of water, except during floods. Horse creek rises in the Laramie hills, south of Chugwater, the various streams which go to make it up flowing out easterly upon the plains. On the highlands in this vicinity farming without irrigation has been attempted with some success, but no dependence can be placed upon the crops coming to maturity every year.

At about the place where the North Platte crosses into Nebraska, and at various points below this, are the headworks of large irrigating canals, some of them in operation, others in various stages of construction. These cover lands on both sides of the river, the greater number of irrigation works being, however, on the south side. In addition surveys have been made for great systems, which, if carried out, will involve the expenditure of millions of dollars. The object in view in these large schemes is to mount the bluffs bordering the bottom lands along the river and thus carry out water upon the plains. These bluffs rise abruptly to heights of 300 feet and over, so that if the project is practicable the canal lines must be very long and expensive. The soil, however, on the plains is doubtless better than that in the valley, being in places less sandy and without an excess of alkaline salts. The valley or bottom lands along the river are being brought under cultivation by irrigation, there being probably a dozen canals already in use. In this part of the Platte drainage basin, however, corn, wheat, and other cereals are usually successfully raised without the application of water.

The large amount of water available in the North Platte renders possible the successful operation of extensive systems of irrigation which can be made to cover many thousand acres of fertile bottom land even if the bluffs can not be surmounted. Measurements of the discharge of the river have been made at various points by the state engineer of Wyoming and also by topographers of the U. S. Geological

Survey. These have been mainly at Douglas, in Converse county, Wyoming, 70 miles or more above the mouth of Laramie river, also at Fairbanks, Laramie county, about 15 miles above the mouth of Laramie river, and at points in Nebraska from near the state line down to the town of North Platte, at the junction of this river with the South Platte. The following table gives the results of these measurements:

Date.	Locality.	Drainage area in square miles.	Discharge in second-feet.
June 3, 1891	Douglas, Wyo	14,665	10,130
Oct. 13, 1891	Fairbanks, Wyo	16,775	579
Dec. 4, 1891	Douglas, Wyo	14,665	807
Nov. 5, 1892	......do	14,665	595
Sept. 14, 1892	North Platte, Nebr	28,250	770
Oct. 8, 1892	Camp Clarke, Nebr	25,267	335
Nov. 2, 1892	North Platte, Nebr	28,250	1,070
Nov. 22, 1892	......do	28,250	1,370

These gaugings show that during the latter part of the year the discharge may fall below 500 second-feet, but even with this minimum quantity canals of considerable size can be successfully operated, especially if they take water from points along the stream at distances of from 10 to 20 miles from each other. The channel of the river and the adjacent low lands are underlain by pervious sands and gravels containing large volumes of water, and even if one irrigating system takes all of the available water at a given point it is probable that at a distance of 10 miles or more below there will be found flowing a stream of considerable size due to the return of the ground water to the surface. The gaugings of this river made by Mr. A. M. Van Auken, mentioned in the preceding report,[1] doubtless give an exaggerated idea of the low-water discharge, and in the light of later official measurements are considered to be misleading. The observations of river height made by him serve, however, to illustrate the relative fluctuations of the river and are therefore given in the accompanying diagram, Fig. 57.

SOUTH PLATTE, ABOVE DENVER.

The South Platte heads behind the Front range of the Rocky mountains, its upper waters coming from the South Park,[2] which in many respects resembles the region from which come the higher tributaries of the North Platte. The Park range, rising to heights of 13,000 feet and upward, on the west and the Colorado Front range on the east receive a large amount of snow during the winter, which, melting, feeds numerous small streams flowing into the park. The altitude of the valley lands ranges from 8,000 to 10,000 feet, and, as a consequence, only a few of the hardier cereals can be raised. Various kinds of grass, however, grow luxuriantly, especially if water is applied during the

---

[1] Twelfth annual report of U. S. Geol. Survey, pt. 2, Irrigation, pp. 219, 240.
[2] U. S. Geol. and Geog. Survey Terr., Hayden, 1876, pp. 323-328.

DISCHARGE OF ARIZONA STREAMS.

GILA RIVER.

[Gauging station at Buttes, Arizona. Drainage area, 13,750 square miles.]

Year.	Jan.	Feb.	Mar.	Apr.	May.	June.	July.	Aug.	Sept.	Oct.	Nov.	Dec.	Annual.
	Sec ft.	Sec ft.	Sec ft.	Sec ft.	Sec ft.	Sec ft.	Sec ft.	Sec ft.	Sec ft.	Sec ft.	Sec ft.	Sec ft.	Sec ft.
1889								115	128	157	212	275	
1890	680	528	387	238	87	28	130	3,137					
Means	680	528	387	238	87	28	130	1,626	128	157	212	275	377

SALT RIVER.

[Gauging station¹ at Arizona dam, Arizona. Drainage area, 12,350 square miles.]

1888								*350	*350	331	842	6,698	
1889	5,947	2,605	8,745	3,975	1,039	470	695	417	521	440	578	5,686	2,576
1890	4,982	10,097	6,421	1,840	914	511	324	3,895	2,319	2,768	4,717	6,250	3,771
Means	5,465	6,351	7,583	2,908	977	491	510	1,551	1,070	1,179	2,045	6,214	3,074

PROSSER CREEK.

[Gauging station at Boca, California. Drainage area, 55 square miles.]

1889				*100	259	110	17	3	2				
1890				340	817	580	382	102	57	42	38		
Means				220	538	345	200	53	30	42	38		183

LITTLE TRUCKEE RIVER.

[Gauging station at Boca, California. Drainage area, 186 square miles.]

1890				956	1,998	1,491	749	200	97	86			

TRUCKEE RIVER.

[Gauging station at Boca, California. Drainage area, 887 square miles.]

1890				637	2,751	5,275	4,291	1,879	736	543	555		

[Gauging station at Vista, Nevada. Drainage area, 1,519 square miles.]

1890				4,496	5,960	4,162	2,196	932	682	742	765	750	
1891	*700	*650	*650	1,523	2,765	1,905	945	483	558	561	563	508	980
1892	593	505	723	854	937								
Means	647	578	687	2,291	3,231	3,034	1,572	719	620	652	634	629	1,275

EAST CARSON RIVER.

[Gauging station at Rodenbah, Nevada. Drainage area, 414 square miles.]

1890				1,026	2,654	2,439	1,789	507	415	386	384	379	
1891	388	402	783	452	1,445	1,328	618	408	388	385	385	438	619
1892	396	388	422	478	1,236	1,158	506	415	414	416	414	1,097	650
Means	389	395	603	652	1,775	1,628	971	473	406	396	395	618	726

* Estimated.   ¹ Data from Samuel A. Davis, C. E., Phœnix, Oregon.

WATER SUPPLY FOR IRRIGATION.

WEST CARSON RIVER.

[Gauging station at Woodfords, California. Drainage area, 70 square miles.]

Year.	Jan.	Feb.	Mar.	Apr.	May.	June.	July.	Aug.	Sept.	Oct.	Nov.	Dec.	Annual
	Sec.ft.	Sec.ft.	Sec.ft.	Sec.ft.	Sec.ft.	Sec.ft.	Sec.ft.	Sec.ft.	Sec.ft.	Sec.ft.	Sec.ft.	Sec.ft.	Sec.ft.
1890	.....	.....	.....	284	657	614	380	135	75	67	49	53	.....
1891	52	48	61	127	534	338	130	65	41	48	43	47	128
1892	45	46	65	.....	.....	.....	.....	.....	.....	.....	.....	.....	.....
Means....	49	47	63	206	596	476	255	100	58	58	46	50	167

BEAR RIVER.

[Gauging station at Battle Creek, Idaho. Drainage area, 4,500 square miles.]

1889	875	809	1,271	2,978	5,199	4,074	1,582	1,000	643	355	487	565	.....
1890	.....	.....	.....	.....	.....	.....	.....	.....	.....	854	783	748	1,751
1891	695	780	790	1,623	2,652	2,245	1,268	835	798	989	957	1,053	1,224
1892	800	855	1,304	1,824	2,710	4,446	2,345	1,025	793	780	687	880	1,537
Means....	788	815	1,122	2,142	3,520	3,588	1,738	954	812	742	728	812	1,480

[Gauging station at Collinston, Utah. Drainage area, 6,000 square miles.]

1889	.....	.....	.....	.....	.....	*800	362	417	569	728	848	1,395	.....
1890	*1,500	*1,000	3,188	4,953	7,924	6,234	3,250	1,754	1,344	1,544	1,403	1,243	2,945
1891	1,000	1,308	1,766	2,739	4,509	3,595	1,502	938	986	1,235	1,262	1,216	1,847
1892	1,202	1,209	2,037	2,397	3,899	5,660	3,037	1,195	1,000	1,131	1,195	1,235	2,097
Means....	1,234	1,172	2,330	3,360	5,454	4,072	2,051	1,076	969	1,157	1,180	1,272	2,108

OGDEN RIVER.

[Gauging station at Powder Mills, Utah. Drainage area, 360 square miles.]

1889	.....	.....	.....	.....	.....	.....	.....	50	52	89	105	421	.....
1890	382	640	978	1,449	1,818	910	458	312	206	265	255	*240	663
Means	382	640	978	1,449	1,818	910	458	161	129	177	180	331	639

WEBER RIVER.

[Gauging station at Uinta, Utah. Drainage area, 1,000 square miles.]

1889	.....	.....	.....	.....	.....	.....	.....	.....	.....	181	208	430	.....
1890	457	547	1,091	2,184	4,528	2,017	549	286	265	333	298	290	1,070
1891	303	461	625	1,502	2,752	1,621	844	338	402	399	373	354	880
1892	599	695	800	900	2,705	2,807	819	239	187	240	357	476	907
Means	453	568	839	1,529	3,328	2,168	738	286	285	338	309	432	944

AMERICAN FORK.

[Gauging station at bridge above town of American Fork, Utah. Drainage area, 66 square miles.]

1889	.....	.....	.....	.....	.....	.....	.....	38	30	33	30	67	.....
1890	62	72	117	*380	*666	*208	*45	.....	.....	.....	.....	.....	.....
Means....	62	72	117	380	666	208	45	38	30	33	30	67	146

* Estimated.

DISCHARGE OF UTAH STREAMS.

PROVO RIVER.

[Gauging station in canyon above Provo, Utah. Drainage area, 640 square miles.]

Year.	Jan.	Feb.	Mar.	Apr.	May.	June.	July.	Aug.	Sept.	Oct.	Nov.	Dec.	Annual
	Sec. ft.	Sec. ft.	Sec. ft.	Sec. ft.	Sec. ft.	Sec. ft.	Sec. ft.	Sec. ft.	Sec. ft.	Sec. ft.	Sec. ft.	Sec. ft.	Sec. ft.
1889							190	145	150	189	224	284	
1890	305	377	519	840	1,926	1,184	314	252	244	304	303	293	572
1891	255	311	492	478	1,226	1,190	423	290	314	364	380	243	503
1892	336	351	361	377	1,079	1,513	441	201	201	241	279	257	460
Means	296	346	457	565	1,410	1,295	332	215	227	272	296	319	503

SPANISH FORK.

[Gauging station at canyon above town of Spanish Fork, Utah. Drainage area, 670 square miles.]

1889									56	62	55	67	
1890	68	76	143	387	777	205	114	64	63	64	50	50	172
Means	68	76	143	387	777	205	114	64	57	63	52	59	172

SEVIER RIVER.

[Gauging station at Leamington, Utah. Drainage area, 5,595 square miles.]

1889								48	53	111	274	395	
1890	625	713	636	726	1,705	1,250	346	153	157	310	373	509	625
1891	735	772	614	509	1,114	905	297	195	175	202	312	551	535
1892	1,016	931	738	232	250	718	88	53	49	50	117	570	401
Means	792	805	662	487	1,023	973	244	112	108	169	269	506	513

HENRY FORK.

[Gauging station at ferry, 1 mile above mouth Falls river, Idaho. Drainage area, 201 square miles.]

1890	1,200	1,250	1,300	1,875	4,580	2,270	1,550	1,456	3,314	1,280	1,280	1,280	1,719
1891	1,280	1,280	1,280	1,516	2,184	1,801							
Means	1,240	1,265	1,290	1,696	3,382	2,036	1,550	1,456	1,314	1,280	1,280	1,280	1,569

FALLS RIVER.

[Gauging station at canyon, 5 miles above mouth of river, Idaho. Drainage area, 594 square miles.]

1890				1,730	3,342	2,706	1,669	971	774	660	541	520	
1891	500	450	450	606	1,765	1,681	1,131	607	520	520	520	520	773
Means	500	450	450	1,168	2,554	2,194	1,400	789	647	590	531	520	984

TETON RIVER.

[Gauging station at Chase's ranch, near Perry, Idaho. Drainage area, 967 square miles.]

1890				740	2,730	2,812	2,130	678	462	475	450	450	
1891	400	465	450	630	1,402	1,661	1,950	547	450	444	*425	*425	696
1892	*400	*425	450	575	1,911	3,845	2,780	758	488	471	450	*450	1,084
Means	400	445	450	648	2,014	2,773	1,987	661	467	464	442	445	933

13 GEOL., PT. III——7

WATER SUPPLY FOR IRRIGATION.

SNAKE RIVER.

[Gauging station at Idaho Falls, formerly known as Eagle Rock, Idaho. **Drainage area, 10,100 square miles.**]

Year.	Jan.	Feb.	Mar.	Apr.	May.	June.	July.	Aug.	Sept.	Oct.	Nov.	Dec.	Annual.
	Sec.ft.	Sec.ft.	Sec.ft.	Sec.ft.	Sec.ft.	Sec.ft.	Sec.ft.	Sec.ft.	Sec.ft.	Sec.ft.	Sec.ft.	Sec.ft.	Sec.ft.
1889						5,184	2,594	2,900	2,425	2,737	2,661		
1890	*2,000	*2,000	2,006	5,702	35,606	34,870	19,970	7,875	4,934	4,552	4,207	3,900	10,635
1892	*3,000	*3,000	3,900	3,760	18,187	41,357	24,069	6,462	4,312	4,156	4,100	*4,000	10,025
Means	2,500	2,500	2,950	4,731	26,897	38,114	16,374	5,977	3,849	3,711	3,681	3,500	9,565

OWYHEE RIVER.

[Gauging station at Rigsby, near Ontario, Oregon. Drainage area, 9,875 square miles.]

1890			6,140	6,558	5,913	1,465	343	179	170	170	221	309	
1891	360	952	3,513	4,984	3,114	1,267	448	332	317	325	376	320	1,332
1892	320	1,250	3,900	13,466	13,082	2,986	948	594	506	570	783	800	3,268
Means	340	1,091	4,451	8,336	7,362	1,883	580	335	331	355	460	476	2,192

MALHEUR RIVER.

[Gauging station at Vale, Oregon. Drainage area, 9,900 square miles.]

1890			2,912	2,770	1,027	254	43	17	15	44	118	83	
1891	88	319	703	511	217	78	30	26	23				
Means	88	319	1,808	1,641	922	166	37	22	19	44	118	83	439

WEISER RIVER.

[Gauging station at canyon above town of Weiser, Idaho. Drainage area, 1,670 square miles.]

1890			5,773	4,792	4,682	1,792	590	138	103	166	222	396	
1891	292	678	2,855	1,777	1,331	703							
Means	292	678	4,314	3,285	3,107	1,248	590	138	103	166	222	396	1,728

ANNUAL DISCHARGE.

River.	Year ending—	Discharge.			Total for year.	Drainage area.	Run off.	
		Maximum.	Minimum.	Mean.			Depth.	Per square mile.
		Sec. feet.	Sec. feet.	Sec. feet.	Acre-feet.	Sq. miles.	Inches.	Sec. ft.
West Gallatin	Dec., 1890	3,800	326	871	630,604	850	14·0	1·03
	Dec., 1891	2,975	370	880	637,120		14·0	1·03
	Dec., 1892	6,800	402	1,123	815,250		18·0	1·32
Madison	Dec., 1890	6,420	1,285	2,068	1,494,513	2,085	13·4	·99
	Dec., 1891	4,620	1,070	1,872	1,354,328		12·2	·90
	Dec., 1892	5,940	1,240	1,844	1,338,670		12·0	·88
Red Rock	Dec., 1890	675	40	148	107,249	1,330	1·5	·11
Missouri	Dec., 1890	12,500	1,742	4,307	3,118,268	17,615	3·3	·24
	Dec., 1891	16,355	1,742	5,503	3,984,272		4·4	·31
Sun	Dec., 1890	4,085	160	715	517,676	1,175	8·2	·61
Yellowstone	Dec., 1890	11,915	516	3,181	2,303,944	2,700	16·0	1·18
	Dec., 1891	8,975	285	2,421	1,752,804		12·2	·90
	Dec., 1892	15,500	390	3,262	2,324,534		16·2	1·19
Cache la Poudre	Dec., 1889	1,900	32	283	204,868	1,060	3·6	·27
	Dec., 1890	1,804	37	355	242,540		4·3	·33
	Dec., 1891	5,060	32	390	283,124		5·0	·37

TOTAL DISCHARGE.

ANNUAL DISCHARGE—Continued.

River.	Year ending—	Discharge.			Total for year.	Drainage area.	Run off.	
		Maximum.	Minimum.	Mean.			Depth.	Per square mile.
		Sec. feet.	*Sec. feet.*	*Sec. feet.*	*Acre-feet.*	*Sq. miles.*	*Inches.*	*Sec. ft.*
Arkansas at Canyon City	Dec., 1888	2,760	430	860	622,640	3,060	3·8	·28
	Dec., 1889	2,620	190	433	313,492		1·9	·14
	Dec., 1890	3,270	180	874	632,776		3·0	·29
	Dec., 1891	4,330	325	1,012	732,688		4·5	·33
	Dec., 1892	4,750	345	889	645,378		4·0	·29
Arkansas at Pueblo	Dec., 1886	7,650	400	1,441	1,043,284	4,600	4·2	·31
	Dec., 1887	6,510	400	1,323	957,852		3·0	·29
Rio Grande at Del Norte, Colorado	Dec., 1890	5,930	307	1,242	899,208	1,400	12·0	·89
	Dec., 1891	5,650	290	1,403	1,015,772		13·6	1·00
	Dec., 1892	4,710	290	812	589,480		0·9	·58
Rio Grande at Embudo, New Mexico	Dec., 1889	5,060	181	1,032	747,168	7,000	2·0	·15
	Dec., 1890	6,671	200	1,467	1,062,048		2·8	·21
	Dec., 1891	8,550	225	1,855	1,343,020		3·5	·26
	Dec., 1892	6,065	140	1,240	900,190		2·4	·18
Rio Grande at El Paso, Texas	Dec., 1890	7,200	40	1,327	960,748	30,000	·60	·044
	Dec., 1891	16,920	0	2,653	1,920,772		1·2	·088
	Dec., 1892	10,050	0	1,285	933,150		·6	·043
Gila	Aug., 1890	6,330	11	503	364,172	13,750	·50	·037
Salt	Dec., 1889	33,794	319	2,576	1,865,624	12,260	2·8	·21
	Dec., 1890	143,288	397	3,771	2,730,204		4·2	·31
Truckee, Vista	Mar., 1891	7,510	400	1,895	1,371,969	1,519	17·0	1·25
	Dec., 1891	3,285	370	980	709,520		8·8	·65
East Carson	Mar., 1891	4,260	375	970	702,280	414	31·8	2·35
	Dec., 1891	1,684	375	619	448,156		20·4	1·50
	Dec., 1892	2,596	290	610	442,636		20·1	1·47
West Carson	Mar., 1891	1,284	42	206	149,144	70	40·0	2·94
	Dec., 1891	740	34	128	92,672		24·8	1·83
Bear at Battle Creek	Dec., 1890	5,980	270	1,751	1,267,724	4,500	5·3	·39
	Dec., 1891	3,060	600	1,224	886,176		3·7	·27
	Dec., 1892	5,260	600	1,537	1,115,801		4·6	·34
Bear at Collinston	Dec., 1890	8,230	1,000	2,945	2,132,160	6,000	6·6	·49
	Dec., 1891	5,000	825	1,847	1,337,228		4·2	·31
	Dec., 1892	6,260	1,000	2,097	1,522,333		4·8	·35
Ogden	Dec., 1890	2,178	215	663	480,012	360	25·0	1·84
Weber	Dec., 1890	5,465	200	1,070	774,680	1,800	9·1	·67
	Dec., 1891	4,555	240	880	637,120		7·5	·55
	Dec., 1892	5,725	100	907	658,446		7·7	·57
American Fork	July, 1890	885	6	186	135,704	66	39·0	2·22
Provo	Dec., 1890	2,260	200	572	414,128	640	12·1	·89
	Dec., 1891	1,704	200	503	364,172		10·7	·79
	Dec., 1892	1,740	200	469	340,475		9·0	·73
Spanish Fork	Dec., 1890	1,040	50	172	124,528	679	3·5	·26
Sevier	Dec., 1890	2,329	150	625	452,500	5,395	1·5	·11
	Dec., 1891	1,386	140	535	387,340		1·3	·10
	Dec., 1892	1,222	48	401	291,110		1·0	·07
Henry	Dec., 1890	7,710	1,120	1,719	1,244,566		25·0	1·84
Falls	Mar., 1891	4,440	450	1,194	864,456	594	27·2	2·01
	Dec., 1891	2,790	450	773	559,652		17·6	1·30
Teton	Mar., 1891	4,445	400	1,921	799,204	957	14·4	1·06
	Dec., 1891	2,368	480	696	503,904		9·8	·72
	Dec., 1892	5,270	450	1,064	765,941		15·3	1·12
Snake	Dec., 1890	50,450	2,000	10,635	7,699,740	10,100	14·2	1·05
	Dec., 1892	54,380	2,250	10,025	7,277,749		13·5	1·00
Owyhee	Mar., 1891	11,230	170	1,656	1,198,944	9,875	2·3	·17
	Dec., 1891	10,000	200	1,332	964,368		1·9	·14
	Dec., 1892	18,000	320	3,268	2,372,436		4·5	·33
Malheur	Feb., 1891	4,445	15	698	505,353	9,900	·95	·07
	Sept., 1891	2,820	15	187	135,368		·26	·02
Weiser	Feb., 1891	11,220	80	1,652	1,196,048	1,670	13·4	·99
	June, 1891	9,300	80	771	558,202		6·3	·R.

dry season. Along each of the small streams, wherever ditches can be successfully located at small expense, irrigation is being carried on and large crops of hay are obtained.

The water supply of the South park is relatively large and is freely used upon the hay lands. In a few instances the number of ditches

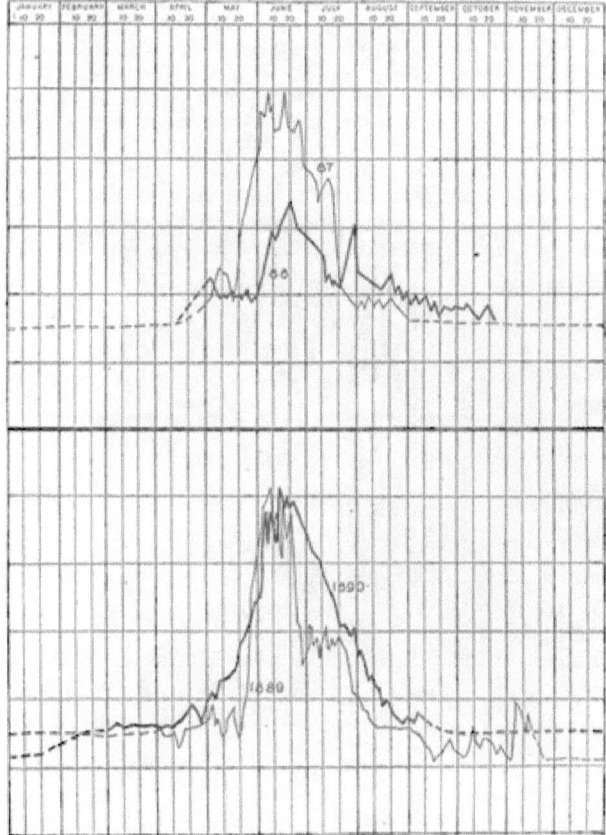

Fig. 57.—Diagram of daily fluctuations of North Platte river, Wyoming, 1887 to 1890.

has been so greatly increased that there is scarcity during the dry season, and it is possible that attempts will be made to obviate this by the construction of reservoirs. In view of the great and increasing deficiency of water farther down the stream it seems imperative to utilize all possible methods of saving water in these elevated regions.

The tributaries of the South Platte in the park flow in a general southeasterly direction, then turn toward the north and pass out in deep canyons through the Front range. A few measurements of these streams were made in 1876 by topographers of the Hayden survey. These show that on July 3 the Middle fork of the South Platte, at a point about 6 miles below Fairplay, discharged 388 second-feet, and at Hartzell's ranch, above the mouth of the Little Platte, on June 29, the discharge was 367 second-feet. Further down, below the mouth of Twin creek, the discharge, on June 23, was 1,015 second-feet, and at the foot of the canyon, on September 8, was 1,400 second-feet.[1] A continuous record of the height of the water flowing in the river was begun by the state engineer of Colorado[2] on July 12, 1887, at a station near Deansbury in the canyon of the river, about 26 miles above Denver, and where the drainage area is 2,600 square miles. The results of the

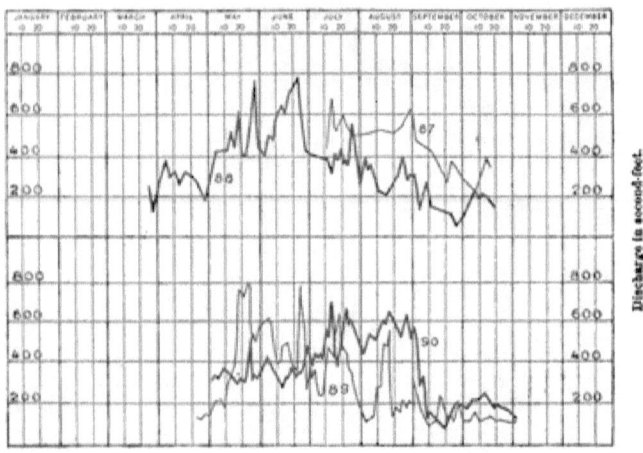

Fig. 58.—Diagram of daily discharge of South Platte river near Deansbury, Colo., 1887 to 1890.

computations of daily discharge are shown in the tables, p. 93, and are graphically given in Fig. 58.

Beginning at and below the canyon and extending down toward Denver are several canals which in size rank among the first in the United States. The most extensive of these is that of the Northern Colorado Irrigating Company, commonly known as the English High line. This extends northeasterly from the river, covering land south and east of the city, and having a total length of 85 miles. Other canals of less size and length carry out water from the river on the

---

[1] U. S. Geol. and Geog. Survey Terr., Hayden, 1876, rept. of Henry Gannett, p. 324.
[2] Fourth Bien. Rept. state engineer of Colorado for 1887 and 1888, Denver, Colo., 1889, p. 63; also Fifth Bien. Rept. of same for 1891, p. 19.

same side below this and also on the western edge of the valley. In the aggregate the capacity of these canals exceeds the discharge of the river, and the question of distribution of water in the dry season becomes a matter of first importance. As a result of scarcity of water there have been losses of crops, the yield per acre being in some years one half or one-fourth that of seasons in which water was plenty.

Below the mouth of the canyon the principal tributaries on the west are Dear and Bear creeks and on the east Cherry creek, the latter draining a part of the relatively low divide between the Arkansas and Platte. Along each of these streams ditches and canals have been built, utilizing the available water, the capacity of the ditches being in excess of the summer flow. The discharge of Bear creek, at a point 2½ miles above Morrison, ranges from 20 to 200 second-feet, averaging about 50 second-feet, the drainage area being 141 square miles. The

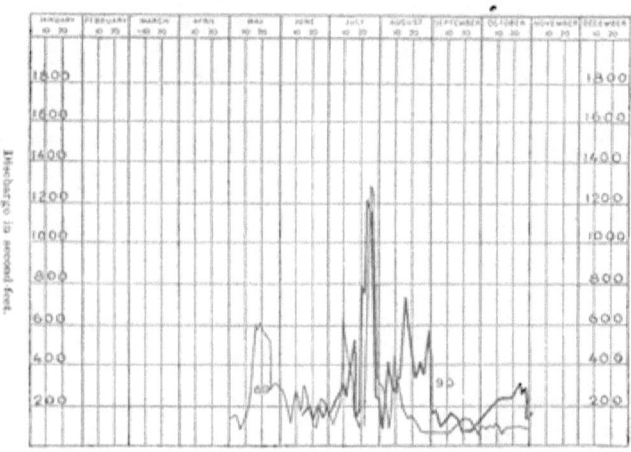

FIG. 59.—Diagram of daily discharge of South Platte river at Denver, Colorado, 1889 and 1890.

discharge in general follows that of the neighboring streams and a diagram of the fluctuations does not materially differ from those given for other creeks.

One of the earliest measurements of the amount of water in the South Platte at Denver is that made in December, 1876, giving 492 second-feet.[1] The total drainage area at this place is 3,870 square miles. A second measurement, made about 2 miles above Denver, during low water gave 204 second-feet. Computations of the daily discharge of the river at a station at the foot of Twenty-first street, Denver, have been carried on by the state engineer, the results of these being shown by Fig. 59.

[1] U. S. Geol. and Geog. Survey Terr. Hayden, 1876, rept of Henry Gannett, p. 324

CACHE LA POUDRE AND OTHER CREEKS.

Below Denver the South Platte gradually trends farther and farther from the mountains, and the creeks flowing into it from the west traverse a wider strip of valley land the farther they are to the north. The first stream of importance below Denver is Clear creek, and north of that in order St. Vrain creek, Thompson creek, and Cache la Poudre, the latter being the largest. Maps showing the lower courses of these streams and the canals taken from them have been published in the fourth and fifth biennial reports of the state engineer of Colorado, and a glance at these shows the large number of canals and ditches leading out apparently in the most confusing manner. As a rule it may

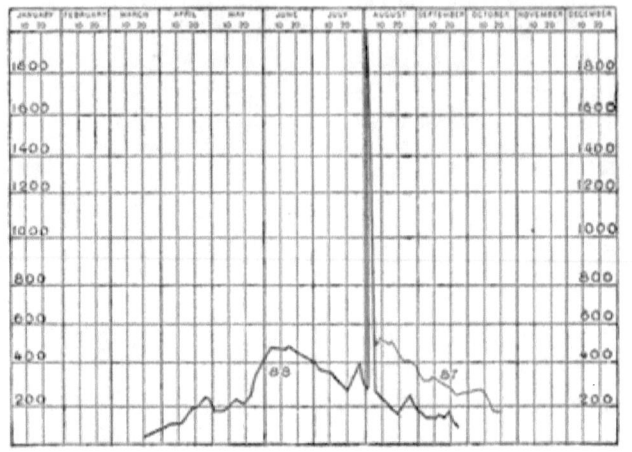

Fig. 60.—Diagram of daily discharge of Clear creek, Colorado, 1887 and 1888.

be said that along all these streams, as well as the main river, the aggregate capacity of the irrigating systems is so great that not all of them can receive sufficient water, and as a consequence only a portion of the cultivated lands can be thoroughly irrigated.

The earliest records of water measurement on Clear creek are those quoted in the Hayden report for 1876,[1] giving the flood discharge at Golden City on June 19 of 1,765 second-feet, on August 27 of 536 second-feet, and on September 3 of 374 second-feet. In August, 1887, a permanent station was established in the canyon at a point about 7 miles above Golden, being thus above the heads of irrigating ditches. The area drained is 358 square miles. From the records kept by the state engineer the diagram, Fig. 60, has been prepared, showing the

[1] U. S. Geol. and Geog. Survey Terr., Hayden, 1876, rept. of Henry Gannett, p. 325.

daily discharge during the fall of 1887 and the greater part of 1888. The most notable feature on this plate is the great discharge on August 1, 1888, when for two hours the river flowed at the rate of 8,700 second-feet, according to the computations of the state engineer. This is typical of the extraordinary floods which may happen at any time, especially during the summer season, on almost any stream of the arid region. These short, destructive floods are caused by what are locally known as cloud-bursts, immense quantities of water being precipitated over a very small area. Floods of a similar character can be seen on many other diagrams of discharge, the relative increase of water, however, being usually less.

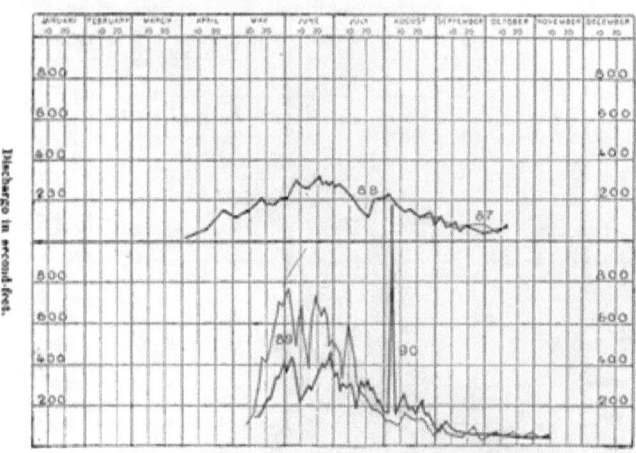

FIG. 61.—Diagram of daily discharge of North Boulder creek, Colorado, 1887 to 1890.

There are fully twenty-five canals and ditches of notable length taking water from Clear creek below the canyon, one of these, that known as the Agricultural ditch, extending around east and south of Denver, while others cover lower lands nearer the stream and follow down along the west side of the South Platte.

Boulder creek, one of the principal tributaries of St. Vrain, is the next stream of importance north of the catchment area of Clear creek. Two gauging stations have been established by the state engineer of Colorado, one on the South Boulder, the other on North Boulder, the latter being about 4 miles above the town of Boulder. The drainage area is 102 square miles. The results of the observations at this latter place are shown in Fig. 61. This exhibits among other facts a sudden flood occurring in August, 1890, at which time the discharge reached 1,200 second-feet. The diagram of discharge of the South Boulder is so similar to others given that it does not seem desirable to reproduce it. The gauging station on St. Vrain creek, established in August, 1887, is located about a quarter of a mile below Lyons at a point below the junction of the North and South forks, the area drained being 209 square miles. Results obtained at this place are shown on Fig. 62, which in most respects is similar to those previously given.

Big Thompson creek, which furnishes water for the lands in the vicinity of Loveland, is in order toward the north the next stream whose discharge has been measured. The gauging station is about 10 miles west of Loveland, being thus, as in the case of other creeks, above the heads of irrigating ditches. The drainage area above this point is 305 square miles. Fig. 63, showing the discharge for portions of the years

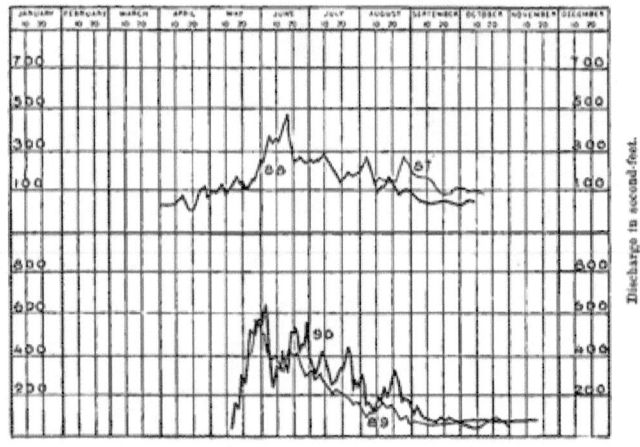

FIG. 62.—Diagram of daily discharge of St. Vrain creek, Colorado, 1887 to 1890.

1887 to 1890, inclusive, has been prepared from data contained in the annual reports of the state engineer. This diagram shows a sudden flood occurring about ten days earlier in the season than that on Boulder creek. These floods, although not discharging what would be considered a large amount of water if distributed during several days, come with such sudden violence that they often carry out bridges and the head works of canals, resulting in loss to the farmers, from the fact that before repairs of irrigation works can be made a large part of the crops may be withered or completely burned by the heat of the sun.

Cache la Poudre creek is the lowest or most northerly important tributary of the South Platte. The point at which it enters the main river is marked by an abrupt change in direction, the river, which up to this place has been flowing in a general way toward the north, turning toward the east in its course across the Great Plains. Cache la Poudre creek receives its waters mainly from the eastern side of the Colorado Park range, some of its tributaries rising near the headwaters of the North Platte and Laramie. It also receives small **streams from the eastern slope of the Laramie hills** not far from Cheyenne. The water measurements on this creek have been made at a place about a half mile above the mouth of the canyon and 12 miles above Fort Collins, being below the junction of the North and South forks. The discharge **at this** locality from 1884 to 1890 is shown graphically on Pl. LXV of the twelfth annual report.[1] From this creek are taken large canals, covering land in the vicinity of Fort Collins and Greeley, the latter place being the locality where systematic irrigation on a large scale was first tried in the state.

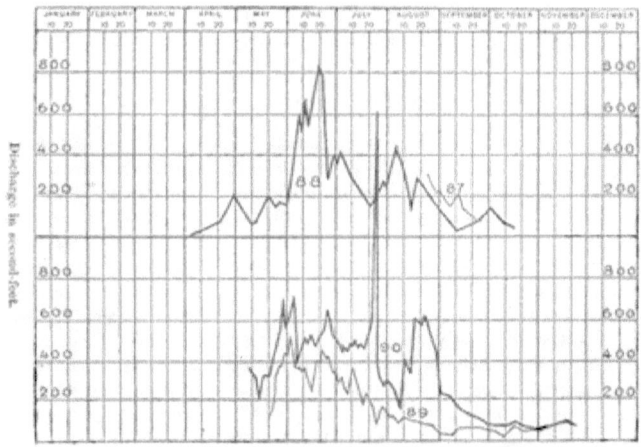

FIG. 63.—Diagram of daily discharge of Big Thompson creek, Colorado, 1887 to 1890.

Besides the canals and ditches taking water from these streams there are a number along the South Platte itself, utilizing the supply which escapes into the river as surplus or seepage. The head works of these are located at distances of from 1 **to 5 miles from each** other, and although at one place **the channel may be almost dry, yet at some** distance below there is **sufficient water to partly fill** at least one or other of the **ditches. Crops can rarely be produced without** irrigation in this part **of the Platte basin, about the** only exceptions being bottom lands kept **moist by seepage from canals above** them. In a few instances these **lower lands receive such a quantity of** seepage water that they have been **converted into meadows or even** into marshes.

The development of **irrigation and the rapid** increase of area under

---

[1] Twelfth Ann. Rep. U. S. Geol. Surv., part 2, Irrigation, p. 258.

cultivation have taken place to an extent such that, as previously stated, the water supply is inadequate to fill the demands made upon it. As a method of relief the farmers have undertaken the construction of reservoirs near the foothills, storing some of the flood waters of spring. The feasibility of larger systems of this kind in the parks and small valleys among the mountains has been often discussed, and movements are slowly being made toward the realization of storage projects. There are, however, many difficulties surrounding the construction of suitable retaining walls and the recovery and distribution of the waters, which as a matter of course must be brought down to the canals below in the channel of the stream, and in many cases past the head works of a large number of irrigating ditches. Without such methods of increasing the summer flow of the stream there can be little hope of extending the irrigated acreage except by more careful methods of applying water to the soil and by greater thoroughness in all other agricultural operations.

SOUTH PLATTE BELOW GREELEY.

After leaving the junction of the Cache la Poudre the South Platte flows eastward and then northeasterly through arid plains toward the subhumid regions. In the eastern end of the basin near the junction with the North Platte, the rainfall is sufficient for many of the cereals if these are properly cultivated. Irrigation, however, is essential for the production of vegetables and fruit, especially on the lower grounds, and even in rainy years can be profitably employed by the farmer. Developments in this direction, however, have been retarded by the scarcity of water, the difficulty of diverting it, and the fact that the settlers can often make a living by what is called "dry farming."

In eastern Colorado the South Platte is often dry during the summer, there being, however, a small amount of water seeping through the bed. Irrigating ditches have been taken out on both sides in Weld, Morgan, and Logan counties, irrigating lands near the stream. These obtain ample water only during spring floods, and having once saturated the land can obtain little or no more during the summer. This one watering under favorable circumstances may suffice, but there is danger of loss of crops later on. The streams which flow into this part of the river are usually dry and at times become torrents, so that it is almost impossible to utilize this irregular supply.

On the highlands drained by streams flowing from the north or from the south agriculture has been attempted, but owing to the scarcity of rainfall has not been on the whole successful. Stock-raising is still and probably will be the principal industry. A few farmers, coming without experience in methods adapted to a dry country, have tried year after year to raise a crop, but without success, and finally, having lost everything, have been compelled to go elsewhere. There is bitter complaint that in the past unscrupulous persons have taken advantage of eastern farmers and have induced communities or colonies to settle upon lands absolutely arid and without means of water supply, or have built extensive canals in the river valley, selling water rights which are practically valueless.

A few irrigating ditches have been dug along the South Platte in the vicinity of Ogallala, Nebraska. These receive water at the time of the spring floods, but during the summer the channel is usually dry and no water can be obtained except that which seeps from the pervious beds, an amount too small to be of any considerable value. As previously mentioned, hopes have been entertained that by means of deep drains extending above the heads of these ditches a large amount of ground water could be had at all times. Large sums of money have been expended in the construction of these so-called underflow canals, but the quantity of water obtained has at best been small relative to the expense incurred.

Much of the land in the vicinity of the town of North Platte is irrigated by a ditch from North Platte river, covering the long, narrow area between the north and south rivers. This locality may be considered as the most easterly in the Platte basin at which irrigation is regularly practiced. Further to the east, in the vicinity of Gothenburg and Kearney, are canals constructed for water power, from which it is proposed to obtain some water for irrigation, but the development of this method of agriculture in a relatively humid region is usually slow. In this, the western, part of Nebraska there are a number of streams which will undoubtedly be used at some future time for irrigation, especially after the results obtained along the North Platte are more widely known and appreciated. Most of these creeks and small rivers flow throughout the year, being fed by springs. On the north side of the North Platte in Nebraska are several such streams tributary to the river and so situated as to have many natural advantages for easy diversion of the water. Among the most important of these are Blue and Birdwood creeks, both of these being remarkable for the uniformity of discharge throughout the year. The quantity of water in Blue creek was measured on November 5, 1892, and found to be 105 second-feet. Birdwood creek on September 24, 1892, was discharging at the rate of 126 second-feet. Besides these mentioned are other creeks of smaller size, having a low water flow of from 3 to 5 second-feet.

TABLES OF MEAN MONTHLY AND ANNUAL DISCHARGE.

These tables give in cubic feet per second the average discharge by months of the principal streams measured by this Survey. Some of these figures have already appeared in connection with other data. The arrangement is that generally adopted in this report, beginning with the head waters of the Missouri and taking the various streams in their order toward the south, then those in the Rio Grande and interior basins, and finally the rivers flowing into the Pacific ocean. There are also included a few computations of monthly discharge made from data obtained by the state engineer of Colorado.

The following symbols are used to denote that the observations have not been continued throughout the month: (*a*) Observations on twenty days and upwards. (*b*) Observations on from ten to nineteen days. (*c*) Observations during less than ten days.

WEST GALLATIN RIVER.

[Gauging station below mouth of Spanish creek, about 20 miles southwesterly from Bozeman, Montana. Drainage area, 850 square miles.]

Year.	Jan.	Feb.	Mar.	Apr.	May.	June.	July.	Aug.	Sept.	Oct.	Nov.	Dec.	Annual.
	Sec.ft.	Sec.ft.	Sec.ft.	Sec.ft.	Sec.ft.	Sec.ft.	Sec.ft.	Sec.ft.	Sec.ft.	Sec.ft.	Sec.ft.	Sec.ft.	Sec.ft.
1889								(b)426	456	402	*400	*400	
1890	*320	*320	(c)320	460	2,092	2,641	1,388	761	607	591	500	*450	871
1891	*400	*400	*450	*500	1,897	2,516	1,534	761	563	587	591	434	680
1892	430	429	400	*450	1,488	4,163	2,544	957	734	743	589	549	1,120
Means	383	383	390	470	1,825	3,106	1,488	726	593	580	490	458	908

MADISON RIVER.

[Gauging station below Hot Springs creek, 4 miles from Red Bluff, Montana. Drainage area, 2,085 square miles.]

1890	*1,200	*1,200	*1,200	a1,620	4,820	4,977	2,518	1,535	1,406	1,498	1,380	1,400	2,068
1891	1,406	1,436	1,621	1,774	3,369	4,167	2,045	1,429	1,369	1,351	1,400	1,337	1,872
1892	1,395	1,504	1,488	1,295	1,454	4,900	3,225	1,519	1,360	1,327	1,424	1,324	1,844
Means	1,303	1,380	1,439	1,563	3,222	4,681	2,596	1,494	1,378	1,392	1,401	1,387	1,928

MISSOURI RIVER.

[Gauging station during 1889 at Canyon ferry, Montana; drainage area, 15,036 square miles. Gauging station during 1890 and 1891 at Craig, Montana; drainage area, 17,615 square miles.]

1889								1,873	2,230	2,502	*3,500		
1890	*3,000	*3,000	*3,000	5,462	10,472	10,078	5,020	2,216	2,352	2,379	2,868	2,763	4,307
1891	2,967	*3,500	*4,000	5,794	9,015	13,645	9,115	4,415	3,078	3,511	3,802	*5,200	5,503
Means	2,983	3,250	3,500	5,228	9,743	11,859	7,067	3,315	2,394	2,796	3,057	2,824	5,229

* Estimated.

DISCHARGE OF COLORADO STREAMS.

SUN RIVER.

[Gauging station at Augusta, Montana. **Drainage area, 1,175 square miles.**]

Year.	Jan.	Feb.	Mar.	Apr.	May.	June.	July.	Aug.	Sept.	Oct.	Nov.	Dec.	Annual May to October.
	Sec.ft.	Sec.ft.	Sec.ft.	Sec.ft.	Sec.ft.	Sec.ft.	Sec.ft.	Sec.ft.	Sec.ft.	Sec.ft.	Sec.ft.	Sec.ft.	Sec.ft.
1889							(a)213	214	200	191	*175		
1890	*175	*175	*175	371	2,804	2,342	961	371	304	315	322	267	715
Means	175	175	175	371	2,804	2,342	961	292	239	257	256	221	691

YELLOWSTONE RIVER.

[Gauging station at Horr, Montana, 4 miles below Cinnabar. Drainage area, **2,700 square miles.**]

								61,669	1,270	976	743	*650	
1889													
1890	*550	*550	5,583	1,417	7,522	10,089	7,682	4,375	2,276	1,473	970	695	3,181
1891	458	*500	316	1,086	5,227	7,592	6,135	3,442	1,641	1,264	801	473	2,421
1892	*500	570	713	664	3,544	11,201	10,189	4,931	2,808	1,555	952	*800	3,202
Means	512	540	538	1,054	5,431	9,625	7,999	3,600	1,999	1,316	889	655	2,846

SOUTH PLATTE RIVER.

[Gauging¹ station at Deansbury, Colorado, below junction of north and south branches. Drainage area, 2,600 square miles.]

1887							*550	350	394	*200			
1888			*250	295	487	552	311	262	179	*150			323
1889			*175	473	460	324	211	129	180				297
1890				391	403	520	502	190	172				374
Means			250	235	452	471	426	306	224	175			329

NORTH BOULDER CREEK.

[**Gauging**¹ station 4 miles above Boulder, Colorado. Drainage area, 102 square miles.]

1887							*110	80	*90				
1888				81	184	261	210	157	80	*80			155
1889					*400	365	277	97	54	36			235
1890					*250	341	258	173	56	33			183
Means				81	271	389	248	134	62	47			176

ST. VRAIN CREEK.

[Gauging¹ station one-fourth mile below Lyons, Colorado. Drainage area, 209 square miles.]

1887							*150	109	*70				109
1888				72	156	320	208	133	56	*50			153
1889					*400	371	197	102	44	39			192
1890					*300	436	292	179	66	45			219
Means				72	285	375	232	141	68	51			175

BIG THOMPSON CREEK.

[Gauging¹ station 10 miles west of Loveland, Colorado. Drainage area, 305 square miles.]

1888				62	132	458	275	190	75	*50			196
1889					*250	382	200	89	49	46			169
1890					*400	530	454	393	151	67			332
Means				62	260	456	309	224	91	54			208

* Estimated.   ¹ Data from state engineer of Colorado.

WATER SUPPLY FOR IRRIGATION.

CACHE LA POUDRE CREEK.

[Gauging station at Fort Collins, Colorado. Drainage area, 1,060 square miles.]

Year.	Jan.	Feb.	Mar.	Apr.	May.	June.	July.	Aug.	Sept.	Oct.	Nov.	Dec.	Annual.
	Sec.ft.	Sec.ft.	Sec.ft.	Sec.ft.	Sec.ft.	Sec.ft.	Sec.ft.	Sec.ft.	Sec.ft.	Sec.ft.	Sec.ft.	Sec.ft.	Seg.ft.
1884			667	219	2,537	4,812	2,144	792	385	6205			
1885				a447	1,419	2,916	1,857	656	272	6293			
1886				a405	1,309	1,673	717	338	185	129			
1887				*208	61	*22	61,401	735	397	175	*120		
1888				181	485	1,113	420	213	109	*90			
1889	151	106	46	113	649	3,338	514	187	67	69	88	64	283
1890	82	79	85	209	1,044	1,280	649	287	103	80	61	70	335
1891	92	79	50	144	1,227	1,960	541	228	138	118	83	79	390
1892	64	119	80	*190	*250	1,512	741	*200					
Means	97	96	69	225	1,193	2,046	924	357	169	127	78	71	452

ARKANSAS RIVER.

[Gauging station at Canyon city, Colorado. Drainage area, 3,060 square miles.]

	Jan.	Feb.	Mar.	Apr.	May.	June.	July.	Aug.	Sept.	Oct.	Nov.	Dec.	Annual.
1888	*400	*500	*600	1,000	1,440	2,000	1,350	632	605	*500	*500	*400	860
1889	*300	*300	*300	300	600	1,374	602	340	229	223	299	335	453
1890	310	363	320	477	2,090	2,611	1,571	670	519	501	522	502	874
1891	431	474	586	857	2,012	3,291	1,468	951	473	624	498	476	1,012
1892	495	493	524	532	1,241	2,787	1,798	769	435	511	527	561	869
Means	387	426	466	631	1,477	2,430	1,357	732	450	477	469	455	813

[Gauging station at Pueblo, Colorado. Drainage area, 4,600 square miles.]

	Jan.	Feb.	Mar.	Apr.	May.	June.	July.	Aug.	Sept.	Oct.	Nov.	Dec.	Annual.
1885					1,069	3,187							
1886	*400	*500	*600	*800	3,046	5,569	1,724	1,481	1,372	*800	*600	*400	1,441
1887	*400	*400	*500	*600	*2,500	3,477	3,352	1,717	1,129	*800	*600	*400	1,323
Means	400	450	550	700	2,205	4,078	2,538	1,599	1,250	800	600	400	1,298

RIO GRANDE.

[Gauging station at Del Norte, Colorado. Drainage area, 1,400 square miles.]

	Jan.	Feb.	Mar.	Apr.	May.	June.	July.	Aug.	Sept.	Oct.	Nov.	Dec.	Annual.
1889									278	319	283		
1890	552	796	487	913	4,331	3,897	1,515	612	383	470	478	565	1,242
1891	990	1,294	1,289	1,416	3,285	4,146	1,093	663	527	844	374	*325	1,403
1892	*300	*300	316	1,047	2,605	2,187	746	444	362	250	360	922	812
Means	614	797	661	1,125	3,407	3,379	1,316	573	391	465	382	523	1,135

[Gauging station at Embudo, New Mexico. Drainage area, 7,000 square miles.]

	Jan.	Feb.	Mar.	Apr.	May.	June.	July.	Aug.	Sept.	Oct.	Nov.	Dec.	Annual.
1889	431	473	784	2,261	3,430	2,922	471	296	212	283	366	542	1,632
1890	437	555	682	2,083	4,966	4,107	1,593	814	545	562	616	648	1,467
1891	586	616	917	2,370	5,965	5,640	2,356	933	489	1,681	778	553	1,855
1892	497	596	1,051	2,979	4,898	3,146	538	194	152	292	317	324	1,240
Means	488	559	858	2,423	4,811	3,804	1,239	536	345	682	520	517	1,399

[Gauging station at El Paso, Texas. Drainage area, 30,000 square miles.]

	Jan.	Feb.	Mar.	Apr.	May.	June.	July.	Aug.	Sept.	Oct.	Nov.	Dec.	Annual.
1889					3,116	2,638	237					71	
1890	196	290	424	2,193	5,771	4,404	804	734	176	65	284	535	1,327
1891	454	809	1,866	4,395	11,852	6,714	2,271	662	768	1,488	341	544	2,653
1892	326	476	752	3,147	7,093	2,945	688	13					1,280
Means	324	525	1,014	3,291	6,958	4,175	1,008	352	296	388	156	238	1,548

* Estimated.   † Data in part from state engineer of Colorado.

www.ingramcontent.com/pod-product-compliance
Lightning Source LLC
Chambersburg PA
CBHW021944160426
43195CB00011B/1219